We Walk Straight So You
Better Get Out The Way

We walk straight so you better get out the way

Denis Hirson

Related titles by Jacana Media:

I Remember King Kong (The Boxer)

First published in 2005 by Jacana Media (Pty) Ltd.
10 Orange Street
Sunnyside, 2092
Johannesburg
South Africa

© Denis Hirson, 2005

All rights reserved.

ISBN 1-77009-144-0

Cover design by Disturbance
Set in Janson 11/16
Printed by Pinetown Printers

See a complete list of Jacana titles at www.jacana.co.za

To the memory of Paul Fischer

CONTENTS

Part One 9

Part Two 53

Part Three 105

Part Four 137

Thanks 156

References 158

Acknowledgements 160

ONE

When we were children we spent our days in Pretoria watching a fat fat hippopotamus getting fatter, suffering from a gaseous form of degeneration and fattening, fattening; we with anxiety at the bursting heart and him fattening, fattening each day, continuing to fatten. What could have become of him?

Henri Michaux

I REMEMBER we were going to be taken to a Sports Day, so we all had to bring sandwiches.

I remember that I was with my friends and the rest of the class in a park with lots of trees and grass. The Sports Day was down the path, with a judges' table, shiny cups and a shotgun.

I remember all the school buses lined up, still warm and stinking nicely of diesel, and the question of where to go and make a wee without losing everybody.

I remember that most of the buses had brought children from Afrikaans schools because our headmaster was Afrikaans. So there were Afrikaans war cries and children speaking Afrikaans to each other but we were small so we were just there to watch.

I remember that at school our headmaster organized boxing matches between boys who had been fighting with each other.

I remember sitting in a classroom and everyone making an "oo" sound, blowing it out as if we were filling balloons with our breath, while I imagined all the shiny balloons in the air above us.

I remember that one of my friends was a boy and two were girls because they were his neighbours. The boy and I used to wet our hair under a tap and comb it, then let it dry in the sun till it was stiff and smooth. The girls were always running off and giggling. One of them was the daughter of a rabbi who collected stamps like me. I wanted my nanny to take me to his house so we could swap our doubles, but they had a big dog so my nanny said she wouldn't take me, finish and klaar.

I remember that there was also a girl called Yvonne, who had long dark hair and big eyes. She could jump higher than any of us on the trampoline, but she kept her mouth open and the teacher made a joke about her catching a fly.

I remember that I was afraid of getting stuck between the springs of the trampoline when I landed.

I remember Yvonne making a compact ball up in the air above the trampoline, while the rest of us waited for our turns. We never saw her again, because something terrible happened to her family. Their house caught fire, or her mother was murdered. Something so terrible that it kept on getting worse.

I remember the way the path dissolved in the sunlight while we were all sitting having lunch. The Sports Day was going to continue afterwards.

I remember the smell of sandwiches in wax-proof paper; soft plastic lunch-boxes the colour of swimming-pool water with ridged lids, and V clips to close them that you just had to press down. Also, the taste of water in a plastic water bottle after it has been in the sun.

I remember that when I was older I wasn't going to run in any races because I was frightened of the noise of the shotgun and also no one could tell me what really happened to the bullet.

*

I REMEMBER when a voice came over the intercom in our classroom telling one of the boys he had to go to the secretary's office. He had freckles and shiny copper-black hair.

I remember going to a cinema in the middle of town with him and some other boys on his birthday.

I remember that before the film, on the stage there was a man who started playing the drums. His surname was something like Blackwell. At one moment he went so wild his whole body seemed to spin like a tornado.

I remember that there was a shipwreck in the film. One of the survivors tried to locate the spot where the ship had sunk, but he had lost his memory so he went to visit a hypnotist.

I remember the boy's father, tall and angular, wearing a tweed jacket, speaking with a clear-cut English accent somewhere in that big rambling house of theirs.

I remember how the survivor started dredging up images of the ship: the deck, a bright sea, a buoy; his dull voice slowly coming back to life.

I remember the boy's mother, red-haired, with cheekbones and big eyes.

I remember her after her husband's death, among the packed boxes in the living room.

I remember that our problem was how to fill the boy's place in our football team.

I remember imagining him and his two younger brothers receiving the news in the secretary's office, looking at each other, filing out.

I remember how they finally found the ship in deep lime-green water; the dim shape of the metal prow.

*

> I REMEMBER how the girls would link arms like birds flying wing to wing. It didn't happen often because usually at break they were doing other things

like cat's cradle or French knitting, scoobidoos, hopscotch or just speaking. Who wanted to speak when there was knifey–knifey and king stingers and Red Rover, all the springs of the body bouncing and the kikuyu grass alive under you like a green trampoline? Sometimes the girls dipped their delicate selves in the red dust of the marble patch, or kneeled across the polished grey concrete of the corridors to play charms or jacks; sometimes they went skipping in twos or threes hell for leather as far as the high empty diamonds of the tennis court fence. Whatever they did, they still always seemed to manage to be back right on time, first in line when the bell rang, effortlessly impeccable in their cool blue dresses with hair gleaming back away from unsweaty foreheads, short white socks trained to stay up at their ankles. But sometimes they just took over the whole playground, one or two to begin with and then more and more, arm in arm, one dress rippling against the next in a pale blue wave as they started chanting "WE WALK STRAIGHT SO YOU BETTER GET OUT THE WAY". Only they weren't walking straight, they were wheeling around; they weren't even walking in the end but almost flying, and if you got out of their way they were already trying to wheel back in your direction to get you. I remember some of the names of girls in my class: Maxine, Lesley, Gail, Naomi, Merle, Ilona, Leonie, Helen, Maureen, Karen, Renée, Brenda. Together they turned in that squealing, stamping, pealing propeller that went lengthening and gyrating across the playground till it almost took off and instead broke into a litter of girls breathing hard against the ground and laughing till their demure dresses shook.

*

I REMEMBER catching moths and then marvelling at the melted gold sheen they left behind on my palm.

I remember the ingots at the mining exhibit in one of the Rand Easter Show pavilions. They were in the kind of dark rectangular tin in which my mother used to bake date loaf. I wondered if they really were made of solid gold.

I remember the big silver shield awarded to the winning house at primary school, and that Alfred got it too often.

I remember Stern's silver engagement rings, and "a diamond is a girl's best friend".

I remember the first time I saw neon lights in Johannesburg, in the house next door to my grandmother's. What surprised me was the plink plink plink when you switched it on, and the way the light polished the neighbour's bald head.

I remember All Gold jams (especially melon and ginger, and fig), and urgently needing the fruit on several labels to stick into my Hygiene notebook at school. So I stripped the labels from the tins before they were opened. They stood in the cupboard naked and silver with glue marks down their silver sides and no one knew which kind of jam was in which tin.

I remember
> I had a little nut tree,
> Nothing would it bear,
> But a silver nutmeg
> And a golden pear.
>
> The King of Spain's daughter
> Came to visit me,
> And all for the sake
> Of my little nut tree.

I remember the Star Chart in our classroom. The best stars were silver and gold. I was very surprised to find that you could actually buy them in shops.

I remember that speech is silver, but silence is golden. I agreed about the silence, but it seemed to me that speech should be something a little cheaper.

*

I REMEMBER the boy who organised a team of minions to help him down at the marbles pitch during break.

I remember how they always managed to get the best spot, with the bushes behind them and a wide long space in front. They would stick up a twenty with great care, scooping up some fine sand and sinking the triangular foundation into it. Then they measured off the paces, traced a groove in the hard red ground with the side of a shoe, and waited for customers.

I remember the boy sitting there, alongside boys and girls who had stuck up castles, or ghoens, or shoe-boxes with mouse-holes that you had to shy through. He was the busiest operator on the marble pitch with his legs open, thighs tight against the seams of his shorts. A rich arc of marbles came raining at him; helpers went scrambling off to track them down.

I remember the boy's face. The elongated grin of his mouth, like a thin wedge removed from the side of a watermelon. The way he slouched across the school playground. The ticking of marbles in his fat canvas bank bag.

I remember his helpers on all fours foraging for marbles in the bushes. There were never any left behind later. I checked.

I remember that the boy was chosen to be anchorman during the tug of war on Sports Day. Teachers stood alongside each team, booming out "HEAVE!" and then again "HEAVE!" as they flagged their arms in the direction their team should be straining. It seemed certain that the boy would always be in the winning team, but he wasn't; after one epic struggle, his feet were brought slowly stumbling forward. The hairy rope wound about him made him look like a captive slave.

I remember him a few years later, standing at the edge of a sports field, facing someone several years older than himself in a fight. He had a flick knife open at his side, and that slovenly grin of his. There were some girls watching; their whispers flamed up in a chorus of dismay. When the other boy, who was almost a man, suddenly hit him in the belly, the air went out of him like a bottle of cool-drink that has been shaken and then had the top flipped off.

*

I REMEMBER my father snoring next to me after he had read me a story.

I remember trying to shift around as little as possible so he wouldn't wake up, even though I hardly had enough place for myself and he was making such a racket that I could not get to sleep.

I remember a story about a poor boy in Naples whose only friend was a dog. The story was in a book with a dark blue cloth-bound cover, a bit frayed at the corners.

The boy spent his time playing with the dog, but one day when he was at school a rich man drove past, saw the dog, and offered to buy it for his son. The boy's parents were so poor that they could not say no.

The boy came home and his dog was gone. He refused to eat. He went around hopelessly calling out the dog's name. Then he fell ill and started wasting away.

The dog managed to run off and reach the boy's house all on its own.

I remember the black and white drawing of the dog, which might have been a collie, stretched up at the boy's bedside; the boy, with dark tousled hair, had his weak arms around its neck.

Then the rich man returned for the dog.

I remember waking up to find that my father had gone, and moving into the warm space he had left behind. It felt deeper than the rest of the bed.

I remember the dogs barking outside. First one, then the next and the next, a whole exploding circuit of anxiety that stretched out into the night.

I remember coming home from school and needing to read the story to myself, over and over, flipping past all the other stories in the book, then skipping the opening pages of the story itself, wanting only to reach the place where it ached.

*

I REMEMBER my father working in the rockery, against the wall below the veranda at the front of the house. He had a hefty pinkish upper half, and his spine as he bent over sat on his back like one of those armoured lizards on a rock at the zoo.

I remember one afternoon I was sitting at the window in the front room and a man was hammering a sign onto the tree outside our front gate. There were big letters that said TO LET. I told my parents. So they went up to the man and there was a scene with sharp voices, especially my mother's.

I remember that whenever I went shopping with my mother and there was something wrong she demanded to see the manager.

I remember trying to work out how far I could wander away from my mother on moments like this, far enough so that no one would think I was her son, but close enough so that I wouldn't lose her.

I remember
    James James
    Morrison Morrison
    Weatherby George Dupree
    Took great
    Care of his Mother,
    Though he was only three.
    James James
    Said to his Mother,
    "Mother," he said, said he:
"You must never go down to the end of the town,
    if you don't go down with me".

I remember that we all went on holiday. We had almost moved into our new house, but after the holiday we had to go back and fetch the cacti from the old house, where we had left them in the rockery. Except that they weren't there any more.

I remember my parents in the middle of a conspiracy, working out what to do, with a phone book open before them on my grandmother's kitchen table like some ancient secret text.

I remember driving off with them, to a place where the houses were so big that when you started coming up the driveway there was only a haze of grass and shrubs and trees, with half a high rooftop on the horizon.

I remember sitting and waiting in the airless car, in the middle of the driveway, all the windows rolled up because of the dog.

I remember the smell of old car seats in the sun, and the way when you were wearing shorts you had to slowly unpeel your thighs from the plastic after you had been sitting there for a while.

I remember the strange pattern a seat could leave on your skin, and wondering if it would ever come off.

I remember that my mother emerged from the house first, with a grim smile and a stride. My father was just a few steps behind her, bearing a tomato crate full of fat-leafed cacti with their scribble of rusty roots sticking into the air.

*

I remember the deep expectant crowds in the middle of town on Rag Day, balconies and flat windows packed, flagstones of pavement after pavement sunk under all the waiting feet as the rough whisper of the procession swelled up and the first floats appeared slowly and solemnly at the far end of the street. I remember wondering what would happen if I got lost among all those wide floral waists and well-pressed grey flannels. I remember the brass band and drum-majorettes with flashy batons and make-up that made their cheeks shine like white chocolate. I remember highwaymen, hobos and cowgirls, cavemen who had walked straight out of *The Flintstones*, hairy babies in nappies, a nurse with the calves of a rugby player and breasts bigger than boxing gloves that he kept on adjusting. Everyone was rattling collection boxes and coins went winking through the air towards them, pennies and six-pences, tickeys and shillings. I remember holding a grimy handful of small change and offering it all up so soon that I had nothing left for later. I remember two St. Stithian's hockey players with laddered black stockings and pig-tailed wigs taking unladylike swipes with their sticks at the coins that came tinkling against the tar. I remember my father shaking his head in disappointment because there was not a single political slogan. I remember the Rag Queen and her Princesses with crowns and bare shoulders and long gloves all ensconced in thrones on their float, waving and smiling permanently; and how, somewhere behind all the satin and tinsel and garlands and crêpe paper, you could hear the patient, muffled grumble of a disguised truck. I don't remember the route they took but I do remember the weighty shadows of the streets and the street-names dour and earnest as one of those old group photographs of men in light-proof suits: Kotze, Kruis, Rissik, Commissioner, von Wielligh, von Brandis, Eloff, Sauer, Plein. But then there was also the gleam of Nugget and Quartz, Fox, Mooi, Twist and Loveday. I remember the "Wits Wits" Rag Mag and an issue with four bald Beatles on the purple cover. It was advisable to buy one or at least fork out some cash and have a sticker marked STUNG on your windscreen. Otherwise sooner or later, that same Saturday somewhere in Johannesburg, a stray character could step forward and stop you with the hungry percussion of a collection box and the red-lipped robot of a smile.

*

I REMEMBER standing with my father in an orange grove in Israel, and being reluctantly persuaded by him that having a barmitzvah really wouldn't be such a good idea after all. His own religious education had been so sterile, he told me, tensing his mouth as if he had bitten into something bitter. The sand at our feet was red and fine as silt. It was winter, and the oranges were ripe on the trees.

I remember the donkey in the field of weeds next to the orange orchard, with its donkey-cry like a saw half-stuck in a log.

I remember boys from my high-school after barmitzvah classes, mocking the teacher, chewing into Hebrew phrases and spitting them out as if they were flavourless bits of gum.

I remember wanting to have a barmitzvah anyway.

I remember the winter holidays, just before I turned thirteen. I was in Durban for a meeting of young people involved in the arts. I must have put myself down as Jewish in the application form, because I found myself staying at the home of a rabbi. His son, Mordechai, had already had his barmitzvah. At supper, they wanted to know when I would be having mine.

I remember the film I went to see with my father, who also happened by coincidence to be in Durban that winter. It was called *Nothing But the Best*, with Millicent Martin and Alan Bates, and was all about a man who gatecrashes a party in a Scottish castle to seduce the aristocrat's daughter.

I don't remember what we did after the film, or anything else about my father in Durban that winter, except that we were going to see each other a few days later.

I remember my mild surprise that our Johannesburg neighbours could hear me when I practised the violin. I was less surprised to learn that they didn't actually like it.

I remember sitting at the back of the orchestra during a school concert trying to bow at the same pace as the other violin players without actually touching the strings because almost from the start I had lost my place in the score.

I remember my special 13th birthday visit to my father a couple of months later, in the back of a Volkswagen outside the Fort in Hillbrow where he was being held under the 90 Day law. There were two policemen with shaven heads and short trousers sitting in the front, keeping their eyes away from us. They only turned around after thirty minutes worth of fumbling words and pauses, to announce that it was time for me to go.

I remember that many years later my father told me, to my surprise, how he had secretly tried to transmit a verbal message to me during the visit.

I remember walking out of school towards my mother's waiting car before the visit. My shoes squeaking slightly on the polished cement of the corridors; that suddenly remote, low din from the classrooms.

*

I REMEMBER driving to Pesach dinners at my grandmother's house, all scrubbed in a white shirt and tie, in the passenger seat next to my mother.

I remember the special pleasure of being out at night, in the dark intimacy of our car, with the lights of the city streaking past us.

I remember the tramlines on Raleigh Street, sunk but still gleaming through the tar long after there weren't trams in Johannesburg any more.

I remember sparks shooting from the rattly tram wheels, and old ladies queuing up to get on.

I remember how ferocious old ladies would become if you accidentally trod on their feet. It didn't matter how much you apologized, you could not appease them.

I remember tureens of tsimmus and chicken-soup steaming in my grandmother's kitchen; the way the sliced pieces of chicken gleamed; the aunt whose favourite part was the neck. She sat at the table holding the thin curved piece of brownish meat in one hand, picking her way through the vertebrae.

I remember the starched white tablecloth with silvery white lines along the margins, and the matza basket covered with a tasselled souvenir cloth showing the Tower of David against a white fake-silk background.

I remember my grandfather at the far end of the table, wearing a clean white shirt and braces, smiling affably amongst my uncles and their families. My mother, my brother, my sister and I sat next to my grandmother. He wouldn't throw us so much as a glance.

I remember thinking that he was the right size to be a jockey.

I remember the thick wooden truncheon that he kept on his bedside table.

I remember that he had lost half a finger in a factory.

I remember the tin of blue mud in the bathroom and its clean chemical smell when he was getting the grease off his hands after fixing other people's electricity.

I remember him showing me his kidney stones in a jar.

I remember him playing patience at the dining room table with Springbok radio broadcasting endless as diarrhoea from the sideboard; walking out across the yard, past the splash of sweet-peas at the kitchen window, to the deep and dusty silence of his work-shed. Or back in the kitchen eating his soup, when there were only my grandmother and me. The little click of the soup-spoon, followed by a slurp.

I remember sitting through the Pesach prayers dreaming that my father would arrive and ring the door bell. He would have sandals and a staff like Moses, and much more hair than either his baldness or prison regulations allowed for.

I remember wishing the bell would ring any second, and my grandfather would have to get up and open the front door for his first-born son. Then everyone would hear my father's voice, and the whole house would fall dead silent.

*

I REMEMBER the moment when we used to arrive at the farm beyond Pietersburg, in the dark.

I remember the flimsy gate of wire and poles that had to be opened; dogs barking, the raw, spicy smell of winter grass, the sky packed with stars.

I remember the farm manager coming out of the kitchen door to help with the suitcases. His khaki safari suit and lopsided boyish grin. Our family sitting down with him for real vegetable soup and bread freshly baked by the dapper cook whose name was Daniel.

I remember that the farm-manager had fought for the Wehrmacht, and been shipped to South Africa from a prisoner of war camp.

I remember that one winter at the farm I was doing a school history essay on the rise and fall of Hitler.

I remember the limerick I used in my introduction:
    There was a young lady of Riga,
    Who rode with a smile on a tiger.
    They returned from the ride
    With the lady inside
    And the smile on the face of the tiger.

I remember the grand old wild fig tree, standing alone at the edge of a field, under which the owner of the farm was buried.

I remember the orange trees, the smell of oranges in the sorting house, oranges in the hands of the black women working there. The sacks of oranges in red twine bags like fat bumpy stockings that the farm-manager used to send us in Johannesburg.

I remember black women swimming in the raised, circular dam. Monkeys screaming softly in the trees. The chewy mineral taste of freshly picked ground-nuts.

I remember Farmers' Weeklies with bloated curling pages in the bathroom.

I remember party lines, and the way the telephone had to be cranked to get an operator.

I remember the movement of the widow bird from one bush to another, ponderously pulling its black tail-feathers along like a suitcase.

I remember the lure of the hill beyond the fields, and the way I lugged myself out of the farmhouse to get there.

I remember the farm manager critically cocking his eye in my direction.

I remember wondering what he thought about the fact that we were Jewish.

I remember playing chess with him in the living room at night, while the farm owner sat with her elegantly raised white hair, reading near the log-fire. He usually beat me easily.

I remember imagining him playing chess as a prisoner of war.

I remember how just once the farm-manager and I carried on playing long after everyone else had gone to bed; the air stretching around us tight as a tent, with only the miraculously enduring, slowly altering pattern of pieces before us. Then I finally made a single, fatal mistake. He looked up at me with his boyish grin, gold teeth showing.

*

I REMEMBER that I was in my room one afternoon when a black man in overalls came to our front gate to ask for some water because he was thirsty.

I remember that our front gate was constantly in danger of falling over because termites had eaten their way through the base of the gatepost.

I remember that we had termites in our cellar, and that the cans of anti-termite poison stored in our passage cupboard stank of a mixture of tar, milk and railway stations.

I remember going to the kitchen to fetch a pale-coloured enamel mug which I filled with water for the man.

I remember our slightly rough-edged grey stone sink, with grooves running along it.

I remember the man's boss, working with him on a storm-water drain out in the street. He also wanted a drink, so I rinsed the mug, filled it and brought it out to him.

I remember his glance as he asked me: "Is this the same mug as you brought my kaffir?"

I remember looking straight up at him and answering "No", then watching him drink the water along with my lie.

*

I DON'T REMEMBER which prefab it could have happened in.

I don't remember how many boys might have been involved, except perhaps one who had pure white rodent teeth and seemed to be wearing shoulder pads, and a second one who was otherwise capable of unexpected gentleness, despite his towering bony height.

I don't remember if they might have used metal-edged rulers, or belts, or simply fists. In the place of the second boy I keep seeing a giant pair of scissors (his father was a tailor).

I don't remember any words. Among my class-mates there was lots of sports talk. Girls and motor bikes. A bit of smut. If they mentioned my father, it was not to me.

I don't remember most of what happened in Science classes either, apart from the intense, exploding light of phosphorus and magnesium in water. Fulcrums, iron filings and Bunsen burners. In Industrial Arts I learned so little that there was nothing to forget.

I don't remember my face being pushed against a desk, or a close-up of graffiti grooved into the sloping wooden surface. The initials of a sweetheart. KILROY WAS HERE. OO7 with a smoking gun stuck through the Os .

I don't remember fighting back. Sometimes I seemed soft as a summer apricot, but my fists could fly. And inside me my unspoken dreams were encased in steel.

*

> I REMEMBER jogging around the rugby field with the rest of the team, studs in the grass just outside the stiff white demarcation lines. I remember the headmaster coming down to appraise us with frozen blue eyes as if we were livestock at the Rand Easter Show. I remember wintergreen and jock-straps, athlete's foot and blisters and being cock-shy, and the boy whose brother was a Springbok even though he was Jewish, so we hoped he wouldn't make a balls-up of the next test match. I remember push-ups, and sit-ups, piggy-

back races with someone bloody heavy on your back, cycling in the air with arms propping your hips. I remember the Royal Canadian Air Force fitness book, and the boy whose pot-bellied father said callisthenics was better. I remember jogging with two or three friends near home, past the serrated din of dogs, leprous trunks of great plane trees, down along the black iron paling of the zoo. I remember inhaling the whiff of dung and fur in the cool evening breeze; the blurred shuffle of animals behind bars, our route edging cage after stale cage. I remember that I fell ill after my fifth or sixth match for Firsts, and was not awarded full red and black striped colours to wear on Wednesdays. I remember the seal cage at the zoo, a moat of dark water circling a gloomy rock, and the seal lying there neatly varnished like molten tar in the sun. I remember the taste of rust in the mouth, sweat in the eyes, the soft and constant whiplash of homeward traffic going down Upper Park Drive. I remember being locked into the pounding pace, wanting only to advance across the flagstones, through the cold-bladed air, the dwindling light, blindly, one flat-soled tackie pursuing the next and then the next.

*

I REMEMBER the furry whiteness of snow outside my window in Johannesburg one morning. I told myself this must be the first time it had ever snowed there.

I remember hailstones thick on the grass after a storm. Biting into them. Rolling them up to make a Hail Man, with bits of grass stuck in the ice.

I remember chips of ice stuck in the cream at the top of milk bottles, brought in from the stoep in winter.

I remember Milky Way bars of white chocolate, white chocolate with bits of coconut in it, and the goo in Chocolate Logs that glistened like toothpaste.

I remember trying to work out why the stripes in Signal toothpaste didn't get all mixed up in the tube.

I remember cutting out patterns in the edge of a potato; the raw smell on my fingers, and then the smell of bright freshly mixed powder paints in which to dip the potato before making potato stamps.

I remember mixing paints to try and get skin-colour right, and not managing.

I remember milkweed "fairies" drifting in the air, with silky fibres and a single crinkled black seed at their heart. Also, the gluey blob of milk when you twisted a green milkweed seedpod from its creeper.

I remember white roots laid out flat under rocks like tiny lacework skirts. Sometimes there would be beetles hiding there that I could add to my collection.

I remember "white kaffir"; "Don't get white with me", white areas, B.J. Vorster's "white by night" policy with no live-in servants. The pencil test. Entries in the Race Relations annual report on the number of people who had officially managed to change their racial category: black to coloured, coloured to white, and very occasionally the other way around.

I remember the second time I saw snow in Johannesburg. Boys from Helpmekaar Seuns Hoërskool crossed Empire Road and climbed over our school fence ready for a snowball battle in the middle of the morning.

I remember that the teacher gave us permission to leave our prefab classroom and repel them.

I remember black school jackets against the white blanket of the rugby field; chaos, triumph and frozen fingers.

I remember walking through our school grounds when I vaguely saw something white and light in the air above me. What I hoped was a snow-flake turned out to be a little pigeon feather wafting down through the branches of a tree.

*

I REMEMBER those wax-crayon drawings when you used many colours and waxed them over with blackness, then used a pin to discover bright threads and patches, like a torch at night.

I remember
    Twinkle, twinkle, little bat!
    How I wonder what you're at!

I remember waving sparklers around in the dark, and the tiny dry prick when a spark touched the skin.

I remember the blood on the tar outside our house after a white man had stopped his car and sjamboked a black man.

I remember the people gathering round and only half trying to stop him.

I remember the business-like way in which he got back into his car.

I remember black pointy leather shoes with elasticated sides, worn with short white socks.

I remember blackjacks, and the time it took to pick them out of socks and trousers after a walk through long grass.

I remember black-eyed susans.

I remember the bleeding maroon-black stain on your hands after you had touched a freshly creosoted split-pole fence, and the vaguely dizzying stink of the tar.

I remember that "Europeans Only" was translated as "Net vir Blankes", and "Non-Europeans Only" was translated as "Net vir Nie-Blankes".

I remember when two black men came in to our house through the back door and sat down to dinner with us. I had a soft boiled egg and started clowning around. One of the men made a joke about the egg-yolk. Then he laughed all the way from his belly, and after that I had to go to bed.

*

I REMEMBER that we had not walked far from school when we saw the woman leaning backwards. There were other groups of schoolboys further along the pavement in that warm after-class daze, a few at the bus stop, most of us with khaki canvas bags on our shoulders, tattooed with names of girls and heroes, guns and ink-splats. I remember the sign at the bus stop: BUS STOP/BUS HALTE, and nearby: SECOND CLASS/TWEEDE KLAS. I remember how few pedestrians there were in the streets apart from us when we came out of school, and that most of them were black. I remember the raw red shale face of the hillside at the top of Oxford Road, and how the buses used to crawl up there. I remember the queues for the dirty PUTCO buses at rush hour, and all the cars with one driver, bumper to bumper. I remember the friend who wished aloud while we were trapped in a traffic jam that all the cars could start moving at the same time when the robot turned green. I remember that it was still early afternoon, and the woman was wearing a pastel coloured apron. She had her mouth open as if she were laughing a wide inviting laugh, although she might have made no sound, it was always so quiet apart from cars and birds under the vast swathe of the sky. She was leaning backwards towards a man who was walking just behind her and had the untied tapes of her apron in his hand. He moved forward to take her by the waist, but she stepped just out of reach, inviting him. My friend said, in that pinched nasal voice of his: "Can't they wait?", and for the rest of the afternoon I thought how they wouldn't.

*

I REMEMBER that the first time I heard Bob Dylan's voice the twang stuck in my ear.

I remember that the first time I saw a poster for a Dollar Brand concert I thought it was a cigarette ad.

I remember that the first time I took a puff of a cigarette I left the circle of boys who were smoking at the edge of a soccer pitch and tried to spit out the taste all over the grass.

I remember that the first time I realized why there was a Tampax in our bathroom I still couldn't work out what the string was for.

I remember that the first time I lay down in a bedroom at the edge of the sea I couldn't get to sleep because it sounded as if someone was sand-papering the walls.

I remember that the first time I went for a ride behind a friend of mine on a motorbike my eyes started streaming with tears and I didn't know if it was because of the wind or my terror or both.

I remember that the first time I really wanted to kiss a girl it was on the beach and instead of touching her I dug a hole in the sand between us until the water started seeping up.

WE WALK STRAIGHT SO YOU BETTER GET OUT THE WAY

TWO

*Above me a white butterfly is fluttering through the air and
a shadow skims through my hands
that is none other than itself,
no one else's but it's own.*

*When I see such things, I'm no longer sure
that what's important
is more important than what's not.*

Wislawa Szymborska

MAY 16, 1973

*One of those many dates
that no longer rings a bell.*

*Where was I going that day,
what I was doing – I don't know.*

*Whom I met, what we talked about,
I can't recall.*

*If a crime had been committed nearby,
I wouldn't have had an alibi.*

Wislawa Szymborska

I REMEMBER the train compartment on the way to my first Commando camp in Kimberley. Everyone with shorn necks and temples. Nervous jokes. Male poker-faces.

I remember one boy in there who had been at high-school with me, and disliked me at least as much as I disliked him. He had a German surname and a bitter lip. We both used to play rugby. Once, during a scrum, he punched me in the face and I had to leave the field with a nosebleed.

I remember that during the medical inspection before being sent to camp we were all shown a picture that looked like a green and blue stained glass window, in which we had to distinguish a rooster.

I remember that, during the same medical inspection, a doctor lightly felt our balls through our underpants while we coughed.

I remember that most of our underpants were white, but one boy in the long line didn't have any.

I remember shaving off my beard in the bathroom on the eve of the camp, with Mahalia Jackson singing rousing spirituals from the living room. Afterwards my chin was strangely smooth, and seemed to have shrunk.

I remember that from the Springbok Grounds, where the army had its administrative offices, you could see a whisky ad on a billboard with a moustachioed gentleman suggesting: "Don't be vague, ask for Haig".

I remember that my things were locked in a green metal trunk. As we approached Kimberley I realized that I had lost the key.

I remember our arrival at the camp, in a roaring truck with wooden plank benches that fetched us from the station. There were many other trucks parked or driving along an endless esplanade with their headlights forked into the night. Dust and diesel fumes. People running. Uniforms. Hoarse orders in Afrikaans.

I remember "Roer jou gat!"; "jou gat", "se gat", "bakgat", "slapgat". "Gattes". And "Don't gooi me grief, hey!"

I remember lying in bed at night during a thunderstorm. The racket on the iron roof, like some form of revenge.

I remember going off to get my trunk opened.

I remember the expression "All on your eis".

I remember that the soup, when I finally got to it in the canteen, was little more than lukewarm oily water.

*

I REMEMBER walking towards the house. I remember the hedge, the low gate, pincushions of grass between the half-sunk slasto tiles with their patches of pewter and rust leading to the front door. I could have been a young immigrant lugging all the suitcases of my life, I could have been at customs when I rang at the door, wanting to enter the country of love. I remember that almost all the paintings in the house showed two people close together. On the grass carpeting at the entrance, a slender twined couple smoothly hewn from a single branch by Sithole. On a wall of the living room a black and white photograph of the woman of the house sitting with her young son across her lap, the two of them fused in a luminous love-wax of exhaustion. I remember the daughter of the house whom I imagined lying in dunes, her blonde hair warm as sun-beaten sand. I wanted her, but I wanted just as much to be where she was, in that family, complete with quiet wise-eyed father, fragrantly laden kitchen table, and self-contained cat. Even when I was not there I was walking there, my steps like a song you sing when you are no longer thinking, the over-melodious, wistful song of impossibility. I remember when the family cracked apart, and the woman of the house packed up and left. I remember walking back to the house. A smell of jasmine near the door; a dead rat on the slasto with tiny insects combing its fur and thin lips open to show whiskey-coloured teeth. I remember standing under the syringa tree to the side of the house, and looking down at the swimming pool where a servant was squatting in the grass, dislodging weeds and tossing them into a tomato-crate. I remember the voices of other servants round the back, clicking like cutlery. I remember that not long before the man and woman miraculously came together again in another country, not long before the son and daughter attained the fruit of adulthood, not long before I had cut my losses and moved on, I was still walking towards the house. As I left it I dug a hand into a pocket, dropping behind me the Hansel and Gretel white stones of hope.

*

I REMEMBER going up in a light aircraft with the girl I wanted more than any other. We were sitting at the back. My rival was piloting, with his teacher sitting next to him.

I remember Johannesburg tilting below us. Rectangles of tennis courts, rectangles of grass, pale blue jelly-cubes of swimming pools.

I remember how, when I was in the army, a light aircraft flew over the camp and another soldier said he thought there was no chance of an enemy plane ever attacking us.

I remember the huge fuss in the army if ever a rifle dropped onto the ground. The strangled screaming followed by dire punishment.

I remember
    This is your rifle and this is your gun.
    This is for shooting and this is for fun.

I remember a school-friend telling me that the army might be boring and exhausting, but it really made a man out of you.

I remember going to visit that girl when I had a weekend off from an army camp, still in uniform. The shorn bristle of my head. The crunch of gravel under my boots outside her parents home, like an extract from a war film when the soldier finally returns from the front. The feeling of being utterly alien to her, and to myself.

I remember the way the altitude of the plane added to the attraction between us, and perhaps even more so the presence of my rival in the front seat, concentrating on the controls.

I remember the heat of our hands together, two sealed halves of a forbidden fruit.

*

I REMEMBER the girl I fell for at her farewell party. She was just about to go overseas.

I remember kissing her while the Beatles were singing *Penny Lane*.

I remember wanting to kiss her again later that week when we went for a walk at night at The Wilds, but she kept her mouth very occupied with chewing gum.

I remember
   I wonder who's kissing her now,
   I wonder who's showing her how
and
   Someone's in the kitchen with Dinah,
   Someone's in the kitchen I know-ho-ho-ho
and then
   I ululused to playlaylay my olololold banjololo
   With youloulou upololon my kneeleeleeleelee,
   But nowlowlow the strililings are brololoken
   Sololo I calalan not playlaylay for
   youloulouloulou.

I remember when she returned to South Africa, and I took her with me to visit my father in prison. The way he asked half-hidden political questions, and later told me what he thought of her answers. During visits it was even more difficult to speak about a girl's beauty than it was to speak about politics.

I remember her lying on the grass, lost in sadness over the man she had fallen in love with overseas.

I remember the attraction of beautiful sad girls, and the need to help them. And the feeling that perhaps if we made love that would help too.

I remember that one night after leaving her parents' flat I found that someone had stolen my little blue Morris Minor, and I had to walk home.

*

I REMEMBER responding to an ad in the paper offering a free ride to Knysna.

I remember the driver. His first name was Hymie, he wasn't more than thirty, owned a Chemist's, and had just invested in his first film. It was going to be romantic, there would be a tragic car crash, and part of the shooting was to take place in Knysna forest. Next to Hymie sat the film director, with a moist rosy face, a well-buttered upper crust English accent and a silk cravat tucked into his open-necked sports shirt.

I remember sitting in the back wondering why I'd been offered the ride.

I remember the film director taking an interest in me somewhere along the way, maybe when we stopped for petrol.

I remember the cosy Knysna hotel that Hymie and the film-director were booked into. I told Hymie I couldn't afford it and decided to start hitchhiking on to Cape Town, my ultimate destination. Hymie offered to cover the cost of a bungalow for me if I would stay on a while. Soon he was planning to drive to Cape Town anyway.

I remember going with them to visit one of the locations for the film. It was a cottage in the thick of the forest, with a couch for a love scene and a heavy odour of furniture polish.

I remember that on the second or third evening Hymie needed to see me urgently. He just could not go on sharing a bungalow with the film director. I had no idea they were sharing a bungalow. Now he wanted me to please change places with him.

I remember that night. The film director lying across our beds belly down, sports shirt unbuttoned to the waist, propositioning me as if I was a girl on the beach. I started telling him about my girlfriend. I didn't have a girlfriend.

I remember hitchhiking off to Cape Town the next morning; arriving at a derelict, flea-ridden house where some friends of mine were staying.

I remember a moment on a Pink Floyd album when a fly starts buzzing; then there are footsteps and the highly satisfying splat of a flyswatter. This came to mind at night while I was trying to save myself from the fleas, which were still a relief after dealing with the film-director.

*

I REMEMBER hitchhiking in Johannesburg, getting stuck in the traffic jam up Oxford Road and thinking it would have been quicker to go on foot. I remember when a car burst into flames at the side of the road.

I remember deliberately leaving my gate just as someone's father's petrol-blue Mercedes appeared at the far end of the road so that he would give me a lift to school. I remember hitchhiking for the first time, right into Hermanus from Habonim camp with a few other boys in one unbelievable go. We entered a tall cool hotel and someone ordered monkey gland steak, so I did too. I had no idea what monkey gland steak might be, but I had just enough pocket money to afford one, which I was glad about because after camp cooking it tasted like heaven. I remember hitchhiking through the Karoo, and a black truck-driver giving me a lift, then almost immediately asking me to take over while he and his co-driver collapsed with fatigue at the back. I remember uncertainly steering that great rumbling mass through the blackness, under the pouring stars, then being drugged by the diesel odour of the cab, and for a deep second falling into a stupor at the wheel. I remember the atmosphere when you were dropped outside a trading store, and there were no cars at all on the road; ragged children and adults on bicycles drifting past, half-looking at you with equal measures of curiosity and indifference, while a hen went on stiffly prospecting for dry mealie grains in the dust. I remember the bugle-brash din of the middle of Johannesburg, after hitchhiking in from the Cape. I remember sinking into a bed soft and warm as bath-water after three or more days on the road; sore bones, fever dreams, and weaver birds bobbing in their boxing glove nests outside my window. I remember being asked to roll a joint by a truck driver, not knowing how to, then sitting on boxes of Appletiser in the back of the truck with a friend, the canvas sides flapping out a rhythm better than Ginger Baker. I remember how the same friend and I were picked up one evening in the Karoo by two men in a big old American car. They were on the way back from a wedding or a funeral in their white shirts and creased black suits; the one in the passenger seat offered us brandy in real glasses that shimmered in the light from the glove compartment as he drew them out. Later, the car made a U-turn to pick up a hitchhiker who turned out to be a tree. Then it was Sunday morning in a small Free State town and the men had run out of brandy. There was no one at all in the streets or the honey-brick houses with their nail-bitten gardens. So they pulled up at the garage where a group of black boys was gathered around the cold-drink fridge. Two of the boys got into the back with my friend and me and we drove to the edge of the veld. One boy stepped out through the tall grass, apparently in the direction of a township. There was no sign of any township. The man in the passenger seat went and fetched a panga from the boot, then sat back down with it across his lap. My friend and I sat with the second boy at the back. There was no one else in sight. A funfair stood off to the right of us, girders and caravans, dodgem and roller coaster sunk against shadow in the heat, the whole place deserted. I don't remember what I thought I was going to do. I don't remember looking at the boy. He was about the age of my younger brother. When the second boy eventually arrived back, he slipped out of the car with no show of emotion. One of the men was plumper than the other, who had a whine in his voice; a sort of Laurel and Hardy team. They tried hard to find a lift for us at another garage before dropping us off at the side of the road and taking the turn-off to Durban.

*

I REMEMBER red ants, suddenly, when you had been lying in the grass.

I remember the red eyes of the mousebirds that used to get to our apricots before we could.

I remember our maid's blood in the grass under the old apricot tree, the morning after she had been beaten by her estranged husband.

I remember wondering if black people's blood was thicker than white people's.

I remember the moment in Peter Brook's film *The Persecution and Assassination of Jean-Paul Marat as Performed by the Inmates of the Asylum of Charenton under the Direction of the Marquis de Sade*, when the nobles are guillotined and someone pours out a large container of what is supposed to be blue blood.

I remember the "reds under the beds" scare.

I remember when American Indians were called "Red Indians", and the chiefs raised their hands to shoulder-height and said "How!"

I remember my father correcting physics papers with one of those red Bic pens. It had finely ridged opaque plastic at the top and a clicker at the bottom that you couldn't stop clicking unless you snapped it off with your teeth first.

I remember having a red tongue after eating red jelly powder or a purply-red one after a stop at the mulberry tree that conveniently stretched over a brick wall on my route home from school.

I remember a painting of a farmyard by Bill Ainslie in which everything, including the ground, a farmhouse and a rooster, is in tones of rust and copper and deep red.

*

I REMEMBER a friend of mine introducing me to a woman at the end of a party, and suggesting with a wry smile that I give her a lift home.

I remember how young I felt next to her, a boy in a young man's body.

I remember the scandal in a Sunday paper about a student I recognized from the campus and an air hostess or travel agent who'd had an affair with him in Italy. I can't remember what exactly was supposed to be so scandalous. But she was quoted as saying he had a body like a Roman god.

I remember that I was definitely just going to drop her off at her door.

I remember everyone jiving at the party. Demijohns of Lieberstein's sparkling white wine. A few black guests. Miriam Makeba singing *Patha-patha*. A swimming pool under the stars.

I remember that the woman seemed vaguely familiar to me. She told me she had been in all the papers after refusing to pay a fine for having blacks living illegally on her property. She chose to go to jail instead.

I remember the cold fear after we'd kissed as I thought of my mother.

I remember having a clear vision of our house, with my mother, my brother and sister each asleep in their rooms.

I remember thinking it would be O.K. to go inside because her husband would soon be coming home.

I remember her telling me casually he would not be coming home.

I remember how empty the streets of Johannesburg were, early in the morning, and how far the mansions stood behind their foliage.

I remember street-lamps with metal shades like skirts, and insects fluttering around the white bulbs with salt light on their wings.

*

I REMEMBER Saturday afternoon visits to my father in Pretoria Local prison. The demure dappled sunlight coming through plane trees onto Johannesburg streets, and blacks walking along unhurriedly. Blacks coming out of Benny Goldman's Bottle Store with paper bags tipped to their lips. Alexander township, shacks and cars stuck in the mud. Then veld behind fences on the road to Pretoria.

I remember not wanting to go. Not on whichever Saturday it happened to be, anyway. Walking to the car with my inner brakes on. Getting into a dogfight with my mother as soon as I sat down in the passenger seat, usually about her driving.

I remember my mother staying in the wrong gear behind big rusty trucks with smoking exhaust pipes, and refusing to overtake. She had only just managed to get her licence.

I remember discovering a letter in the glove-compartment, in which either my mother or my father wondered where they had gone wrong in my upbringing.

I remember the smell of naartjies in the car as I was peeling them for both of us, making a thinly visible vapour cloud in the overheated air.

I remember that I was glad to see the sign for Halfway House, though the second half of the journey seemed even more interminable than the first.

I remember arriving at the prison, just around a bend in the road. It did not seem to be a part of Pretoria. It did not seem to be a part of anything else. It was nowhere, surrounded by a high brick wall, with guards moving around on the ledge at the top.

I remember the smell inside, like a mixture between a stale pub and a geriatric ward.

I remember the tiredness that hit me in there.

I remember my father's slight shock during a prison visit when he learnt how much my mother liked the Beatles, and the secret feeling of triumph that I had won her over.

I remember afterwards, when visits were over, thinking I had had a lot to say to my father, and nothing had been said.

*

I REMEMBER them as if they had arrived together in a procession through the streets but there was no procession, and they were no longer together. Instead, they appeared one by one with years of absence between them, all in ill-fitting drab autumn-coloured clothes apart from the last one who had just been swimming, looking trim though I wondered about the scar down the side of his face. I remember the second one sitting on the lawn at the Union Buildings and making joke after quick joke with the bright feminine needle of his voice as if trying to stitch himself back into the air. The third one was in a house that was much too big for him and another one was with his son in a cluttered room somewhere on the Rand. I remember meeting the girlfriend of the last one, she was in a swimming pool, but not the same pool he later swam in. She was wearing a bikini, and the water that glazed her body was filtered and clean, but like all of us she had been to visit and come back marked with the sterile neon-scorched air and dead metal sounds, the stagnant swamp-whiff of prison that all the Jeyes Fluid in the Transvaal could not wash away. I remember the first one, arriving at the flyscreen of our front door one night. What was he doing there, freed years before his official time was up, without any warning? He sat on the Morris settee that my father and I had once gone hunting for at an auction sale, dipping biscuits into his tea, apparent proof that prison was no more than a car-ride away. I hardened against him, not wanting him to bring my father's presence so close, there was no way to cross such utterly insurmountable closeness, far easier to bandage the wound with distance. I remember the last one standing up from the slasto at the side of the pool while the water mark left behind him on the warm tiles faded like a shadow with a slow life of its own. I remember wives and daughters and sons like myself all witnessing the procession of those who had finally emerged into the light, husbands of women who had been taken too. There was one son with far blue eyes, an open smile that you could sink through and a quiet strength that made you want to reach out to him. He died before his father died Inside, and so he could not follow the procession, which was not a procession, of exiles who had never left and outcasts who had been kept within, lost cases and rebels and ideologues and followers, whites who were just a little less White. All had been recently unwrapped from the dull pigment of a prison cell, the drained habit of absence; dazed and suspended, they looked slowly about them, still dreaming of a country whose colours were hidden as the inside of a root.

*

I REMEMBER going to see plays by Athol Fugard in one Johannesburg theatre after another: the Arena, the Bantu Men's Social Centre in Dorkay House, the Wits Great Hall (*No Good Friday*), the new Wits Theatre, a big room somewhere else at Wits where at least part of the audience sat on the floorboards (*Sizwe Banzi is Dead*), the Brian Brooke theatre I think (*People are Living There*), and the Market Theatre. There was also another theatre where I saw *Hello and Goodbye* for the first time with Molly Seftel playing Hester opposite Fugard's Johnny. I wasn't going to miss a single play.

I remember the new feeling that something urgent was happening on the stage, beyond a curtain of silence at the edge of our lives.

I remember an extract from Fugard's diary when he is working on *Hello and Goodbye*. He has come back from a walk through Port Elizabeth and he writes something like "Today I saw Johnny".

I remember him telling me that he had placed the lip of a wineglass against a wall in a hotel so that he could overhear what was being said in the next room.

I remember when Fugard and Yvonne Bryceland decided to do *Boesman and Lena* without make-up at the Arena. Their faces seemed to be completely naked.

I remember Yvonne Bryceland on the stage at Dorkay House, struggling with a chair as if it was her own body that she could not get to stand still. The stabbing of metal chair legs against the raw concrete floor. Her staccato breathing.

I remember her down on her knees with Athol Fugard, pushing toy cars with toy car burbling lip noises across the semi-darkness of the stage. This was their play about John Harris, and I could not grasp it fully although their movements invaded me.

I remember the photographs of disaster at Park Station, and the victims, one of whose names was Koekemoer I think. The impossibility of imagining John Harris walking to the gallows, though it was reported that he had sung "We shall overcome" on the way there, and it was possible to imagine the song being sung to the end.

I remember the way Yvonne Bryceland moved, from the gut. The gap between her front teeth. The crackling chestnut light in her eyes.

I remember when I was watching *Master Harold and the Boys* and a young black spectator sitting in front of me breathed in sharply and said "Haai" when Master Harold spat in Sam's face.

I remember the accents, as if the actors had spat out all the hot Empire porridge in their mouths and could speak just like everyone else.

I remember being with a group of people including Athol Fugard and Barney Simon in a Hillbrow flat one night. Barney Simon told a story about looking out of the window of a New York apartment in the middle of a broiling summer. Down in the alleyway there was a man who slipped his penis out of his pants and urinated; the sunlight caught the stream of urine as it rolled along. The story was so palpable that the sun could have been beating down outside in the dark.

I remember that Fugard couldn't get a passport.

I remember him fishing near his home, standing in his stocky way, immobile, watchful as if he might receive a blow any moment, wrestling with the movement of the sea.

*

I REMEMBER skipping the pages of poetry magazines when I came to Wopko Jensma's work, and how long it took me to take in what he was saying. The words were too sparse for me, afflicted with a kind of poverty. But inside the poverty there was a code that I needed to crack.

I remember
   i hope to live to the age of sixty
   i hope to leave some evidence
   that i inhabited the world
   that i sensed my situation
   that i created something
   out of my situation
   out of my life
   that i lived
   as human
   alive
   i

I remember going to visit a friend's house and finding Wopko Jensma there. One of his framed paintings was leaning against a wall. It showed a child-like rendering of a girl's face, and she was smiling. He was also smiling. Both smiles were too wide, as if they had been pegged on each side to keep the mouth from dropping.

I remember his drawings of animals, like liquid black jokes left behind by a nightmare.

I REMEMBER passing white foremen sitting in the shade while teams of blacks did work on the roads, and repeating Jensma's words to myself like a caption: "darem harde werk om gat op klip te sit."

I remember that whenever I asked after him, he had drifted off somewhere else. Botswana. Valkenberg. The Salvation Army Centre in Hillbrow. I went to find him there on one visit back to South Africa, but he had already drifted on, and this time no one heard news of him again.

I remember coming across him at a party. Almost everyone was out on the patio corkscrewing to the jive beat of a live black band. Half a head higher than anyone else, heavy-framed owl-sized glasses masking the top half of his face and straggly fuzz across the bottom, he was not so much dancing as tiptoeing from one foot to the next, with slow urgency, like a latecomer trying to find out why there was such a crowd gathered there that night.

*

I REMEMBER the way my bedroom door had to be sealed shut while I was writing.

I remember how we all said there was no great South African novel, and wondered who was going to be the one to write it.

I remember that I used to come home and put on a Shostakovitch concerto loud enough to fill the house.

I remember the light on the garden outside, while inside the long dark notes trembled and crashed. Then I went into my room to write.

I remember how a friend of mine arrived at the front door one afternoon. He was wearing a tee-shirt and jeans, and I could see the sweat-stains under his arms. His face was filled with colour and his eyes were bright. I hadn't seen him for weeks.

I remember him stepping into the closed atmosphere of the living room like a gatecrasher.

I remember that he had had an Experience, he had been in a bus in New York and the city had suddenly turned gold before his eyes. Later, he felt he could see into the soul of everyone he saw in the street.

I remember how his mother used to buy dozens of glass demijohns of Mitz orange juice and store them in the kitchen.

I remember watching his father on the phone during a business conversation. The way his jaws snapped shut just after he shouted, like an animal trap.

I remember my friend using yarrow stalks to throw the *I Ching* at the bottom of his parents' garden, near the swimming pool.

I remember how we used to play mini-golf down there.

I remember how much breath you needed to read Alan Ginsberg's *Kaddish* aloud, and how people started writing "&" instead of "and".

I remember small *City Lights* books with black and white covers.

I remember my friend arrived with an L.P. that he had to put on. It was *Working Man's Dead* by The Grateful Dead, with Jerry Garcia singing

God damn, well I declare,
Have you seen the like?

I remember how he stood there, listening and singing, absorbing the music into his body.

I remember the fresh smell of his sweat.

I remember a picture I had on my wall, from the National Geographic, of a dark-haired, almond-eyed gypsy girl.

I remember Joni Mitchell singing *Wild Things Run Fast*.

I remember having erotic dreams that night.

*

I REMEMBER the foyer of the John Moffat Fine Arts Block at Wits the morning after a cocktail party: on the tables, tens of wine glasses, some of them still glazed with a rose lick of wine. Amongst them, a bronze statuette of a muscle-bound bull.

I remember attractive girls in the Fine Arts workshop, wearing aprons, stripping masking tape from hard-edged acrylic paintings.

I remember one of them explaining Monet's water-lily paintings to me in the library towards evening, the constellation of light across the darkness of the pool. Then we walked out together into the rain.

I remember her finding some pieces of white paper that had been scattered across a road. They had random muddy tyre-prints across them that she was going to use in a painting.

I remember going to a party with her. They were playing a record by The Band over and over, with Rick Danko singing: "If your memory serves you well".

I remember that her perfume made me feel nauseous. Or maybe I was plagued with thoughts of her boyfriend, who was my friend too, and was overseas at the time.

I remember the whole debate about whether to stay on in South Africa or not, and the feeling that leaving would be a kind of betrayal.

I remember letters from people who had left and were busy discovering new countries, new lovers, therapists and poverty.

I remember going with the girl to a sit-in that turned into a lie-in at the bottom of the Student Union Building.

I remember sitting with her on the grass near the Fine Arts Block, with yelps from the swimming pool down below, watching how a pigeon stretched its chest and heavily beat its wings before taking off from a low wire fence.

I remember a concert on campus with cloud-shaped cardboard cut-outs suspended from the ceiling, slowly turning before the musicians. The clouds had fragments of musical scores written across them; the musicians played what they glimpsed with great intensity.

*

I REMEMBER the blocks of shadow from the buildings in the middle of town when we went on the march. I remember the warped echo of our voices, the placards but not exactly what we were protesting against that time, the ad for ballroom dancing on the glass door to an office block. I remember black workers in white shirts looking down at us from offices, and venetian blinds, and the fear when the first police appeared in their slate-coloured safari suits. I remember that nearly everyone I knew was there. I had not really wanted to be with them, I had a headache, but a highly attractive girl walked past me on her way off campus while I was on my way in. She was already on the march and then I was too, out past Pop's Café, over the railway-bridge and into town. I remember that she held my hand but everyone was holding hands so it didn't count. I remember that at one moment I was detached from the march and could simply have been a bystander but decided I had to join in at the last minute and next thing we were being ushered into John Vorster Square as if it had been our destination all along. A prisoner let down a tin at the end of a string with a note in it that read "Got any smokes?" I remember previous protests "in dignified silence" outside Wits with "CHARGE OR RELEASE" stickers, the Archie Mafeje affair, and the time when a group of people including Winnie Mandela was freed only to be immediately re-arrested. Then we were out on our side of the Jan Smuts Avenue pavement all over again, like marathon runners toeing the line for a race that would never begin. The car-drivers were rising up the hill without a blink in our direction except once in a while when a window was rolled down and insults came spewing out. I was standing next to the same girl again. I remember the wishful feeling that somehow if a girl would let you jump into bed with her then sooner or later the two of you might just fall in love. I remember that the question of love was even more mysterious than the question of how to get her to jump into bed with you, but not nearly so urgent. I remember Erich Segal's *Love Story* that the girl was studying in Psychology II or III, and the film with Ali MacGraw who looked a bit like her. I remember that she was in deep conversation with the man on the other side of her who was a philosophy lecturer, but when I looked around again he had gone. I remember that feeling when other people left in the middle of a protest and you wondered if you should too. I remember that she told me he had gone home to make a chair. The protest eventually came to an end but the chair stayed on in my mind. I saw its lines drawn cleanly against shavings and sawdust, in a workshop somewhere out in the leafy suburbs. It stood there in its newly polished repose, ready to be useful, light from the garden streaming against the deep grain of the yellow wood, beeswax raising a swarm of fragrance into the air.

*

I REMEMBER the Ashram we went to, somewhere out in the country not too far from Johannesburg.

I remember the river, and people with lots of hair and flowing clothes gazing into it in a state of very spiritual meditation.

I remember everyone telling each other how far they had gone up the chakras after group meditation. If you saw red with your eyes closed then you were still quite carnal. But at least one very carnal girl said she had reached the summit, which was pure white.

I remember the problem of doing headstands when the ground was so bumpy, and people slowly beginning to keel over after the first few minutes like the masts of a ship.

I remember bright red birds in the reeds of the swamp towards sunset.

I remember when a husband dropped his wife off at the Ashram, and she wasn't as keen on the yoga teacher as the yoga teacher thought she would be.

I remember how he spoke with an acquired Indian twang.

I remember that book *Don't Push the River, it Flows by Itself*.

I remember that other book *I Never Promised You a Rose Garden*.

I remember that it was Christmas, and I had to leave the Ashram to visit my father in Pretoria Local Jail. I went with my mop of hair. Coppery brown beard and moustache. Sandalwood bangle. The works.

I remember my mother glancing at me in very silent consternation.

I remember that some of my recently arrested friends were being held in the same prison, not too far from him.

I remember that when they were let out on bail, some of them did yoga too.

I remember one of Gandhi's maxims: "Chew what you drink and drink what you chew".

One afternoon a group of us from the Ashram went out for a walk through the veld. We came across a newly built house, with raw concrete walls and arches, and a gate made of tall spiked iron bars. No one was in. There was no garden, just the veld dug away from the walls. But just outside in the rusty spikes of grass there was an unattended flock of sheep.

I remember standing there watching the sheep who were watching us through the slots of their eyes, their bodies entirely immobile while their jaws went on chewing.

*

I REMEMBER we had to bring some flowers with us when we were initiated into Transcendental Meditation. The weather was cold, and the best I could find at a florist was a bunch of stiff-petalled blue irises which I did not like at all.

I remember taking them home afterwards. They stood in a transparent glass vase with their malignant tongues sticking out and steadfastly refused to perish.

I remember Alpha waves. Falling asleep in the middle of meditation. The mantra I wasn't supposed to share with anyone, that turned out to be exactly the same as the one a girl secretly shared with me.

I remember the girl who said her eyelids felt like broken glass when she closed them to meditate.

I remember when Tom Courtney's glasses are smashed during a protest in *Doctor Zhivago*, and some substance, maybe iodine, is poured onto the wound on his face.

I remember when I thought that a Molotov Cocktail was a kind of drink.

I remember when there were photographs and posters all over the place of Yevtushenko reading his poetry with a fist raised in the air.

I remember the Blue Meanies in *Yellow Submarine*, and a girl I knew who took strange pleasure in imitating the twisted, effeminate voice of their leader.

I remember when it was in for girls to wear blue overalls.

I remember when everyone was smoking bidis; their bluish smoke and eucalyptus aroma.

I remember the cover of Joni Mitchell's record *Blue*, and her voice willing and lithe as a woman's arm around a lover, singing "I could drink a ca-ase of you-ou-ou-ou-ou-ou, darling".

I remember blue balls, and a doctor gently explaining what to do about them.

*

I REMEMBER writing the word "green" over and over, among doodles on note-pads, in the margin of exercise books and lecture notes. I always used careful draftsman's lettering, as if the word was a label for an architectural drawing.

I remember Leonard Cohen singing
    I lit a thin green candle,
    To make you jealous of me.

> But the room just filled up with mosquitoes,
> They heard that my body was free.

I remember Trini Lopez singing "Green, green". Robust sports players with good teeth wearing "the green and gold". Beetles with green backs like velvet gems. Green aloe glue when you broke a leaf. Green blood of hairy caterpillars. Rita Tushingham in *The Girl with Green Eyes*.

I remember the hot green mango chutney given to my mother by grateful patients at Coronation Hospital.

I remember being invited to a friend's farm, and seeing a slaughtered sheep that had been cut open. The half digested khaki-green grass in the intestines.

I remember our greengage tree, and the unripe fruit hanging from the branches on the day that my father arrived back home from jail.

I remember the green in the eyes of the girl I was in love with, just as it was in her father's eyes. The way the suitors of his four daughters had to brave him as he presided with a fine booming feudal voice over Sunday lunch.

I remember trying to eat the peas gracefully.

*

I REMEMBER when suddenly a number of women started going off to a farm in the Western Cape. The grass was very green in the valley down there, it seemed, and the sky was very clean.

Those who travelled there were soon busy falling in love with other women. They all wore trousers. I saw some of them back in Johannesburg, with flushed faces and a gleam in their eyes. One apparently had a nasty mining magnate for a father. Her skin was like blushing porcelain, and it was even more tempting to touch her because she was out of bounds.

I remember one of them singing
>   My money comes and goes
>   And rolls and flows and rolls and flows
>   Through the holes in the pockets in my clothes.

I remember Monica Wittig's *Les Guérillères* being passed around. You just had to open it and you got a whiff of women with lots of flesh and tension moving around in a tribe.

I remember one of my friends being verbally battered by several women for describing their gatherings as "a gaggle of breasts and vaginas".

I remember that there were also men on the farm, but the women saw them as a kind of sub-caste. They worked in the fields, it was said, and you could tell by their half-erect penises that they were in a constant state of frustration.

There was also another man, one who kept himself apart and slept in the stables, near the horse. One of the women fell in love with him and with the horse, and spent her days and nights riding both of them.

Then all of a sudden it was over. One evening most of them were sitting around the edges of a bare room in Johannesburg, as if they'd had to roll up the decor of the farm, pack their love and leave. Some were still glowing, others intensely quiet and dejected. A few were on their way overseas. The waves were already lapping at the door.

*

I remember the woman who always used to wear fishnet tops. She worked at a bookshop near the campus, and caught one of my closest friends.

I remember how I was attracted to the same women as he was, but not this time.

I remember her coming up behind me as I was leaving the library on campus. She put her hands over my eyes and said "Guess who?" Hopefully, I mentioned the name of the girl I had been daydreaming about, but I was wrong.

I remember Jim Morrison singing "I'm a spy in the house of love".

I remember *Spy versus Spy* in *Mad Magazine*.

I remember following the court case after Special Branch spies had climbed a tree to see into a house that one of our lecturers had entered with an Indian woman. And imagining what they might have seen.

I remember the whole problem of trying to identify the spies on campus. No one ever seemed to doubt that there were spies on campus. The list of suspects lengthened by the day. Most were whites, and not from the posh suburbs. One was from South West Africa. All were male. Some were black, from among the small clique that hung around on the library lawn though they could not register for classes, wearing slick clothes and sunglasses even in winter.

I remember spies behind Afrikaans newspapers in Volkswagens parked not too far from certain houses. And an article in the Sunday press about a student whom the cops had tried to bribe into becoming a spy.

I remember the woman in her room, in a Braamfontein flat: beanbag; stolen red construction-site lamps; mattress on the floor; fishnet top.

I remember that her family had immigrated to South Africa from Hungary after 1956.

I remember that my friend happened to be in London years later, at an anti-apartheid protest on Trafalgar Square. A woman came out of South Africa House with an official, the two of them locked in earnest conversation. "Guess who?" he said.

*

I REMEMBER going off in a car to visit my friends who had skipped the border, and were now in Botswana. I wondered if anything might happen between me and the girl who was driving.

I remember that nothing did happen, though I kept my hopes up till the end.

I remember the simple caravans our friends were staying in, not far from the border. Walking along a sand path with one of them in the sunlight. The feeling that we were at the edge of the world, and that I might lose them for a long time.

I remember the story of their escape. A car ditched at the border. Bush, thorn, mud, fences, the sound they thought was the cops coming after them but which turned out to be cow bells.

I remember the self-righteous front-page newspaper article criticizing them for jumping bail instead of standing trial and proving their innocence.

I remember driving one of the escape cars back to Johannesburg, alone, in the dead of night. It was a little Ford Anglia. The sand road out of Botswana was thick with mud and the car started swerving from one edge to the other. Later, when I had finally made it onto South African tar, I managed to get lost.

THREE

*no whiteness (lost) is so white as the memory
of whiteness*

William Carlos Williams

*I looked in my heart
black blood of history   still not dry*

Robert Berold

*Just then, Pig arrived.
"Where are you from?" he asked Rat angrily.
"From everywhere and nowhere," replied Rat calmly.
"Well, why don't you go back?" cried Pig. "You've no
business here".*

Max Velthuijs

I REMEMBER the sunlight pouring down on Paris during my first spring there, and the strange sight of people sitting three or four tables deep on the bistro terraces, surveying the passers-by in a way that made me think of ancient Romans at the Colosseum.

I remember walking through the streets of Paris making a mental note of where and how I had acquired each article of clothing I was wearing.

I remember the sudden sensuality of girls with delicate unclothed arms and necks, still untouched by the sun after months of coats and scarves.

I remember when it was fashionable for girls in Paris to wear white bobby socks.

I remember the concierge's two children playing in the park opposite my flat one sweltering summer. They stood with flexed knees before the pale blaze of the sandpit, counted to three and dived in.

I remember the beginning of the song "Paris, c'est une blonde".

I remember how the inside of a baguette seemed light as foam under the crust. And how strange it seemed that at about four o'clock children should eat blocks of chocolate inserted between two slices of baguette.

I remember the poster in the Metro carrying the warning "FOR THE SAKE OF YOUR HEALTH, DO NOT DRINK MORE THAN ONE LITRE OF WINE A DAY".

I remember when pale red dust from the Sahara was blown across parked cars in my neighbourhood. And the four red paving stones on the cobbled street facing the one-time woman's prison on rue de la Roquette, where the guillotine had once stood.

I remember that during the French Revolution they had to move the guillotine to the outskirts of Paris because the ground was saturated with blood and the stench had become unbearable.

I remember the May '68 slogan "Sous les pavées, la plage", and seeing the beach sand under the cobblestones when workers began pulling them up all over the place.

I remember realising that nearly all the people in the first procession I saw on 1st May were white: almost the only blacks were the dustmen, right in front, thumping out a rhythm on their dustbins.

*

I REMEMBER sitting in the living room of a house in Johannesburg, surreptitiously paging through a book of black and white photographs of Paris. I paused for a long time over scenes from the Folies Bergère dressing rooms, with nonchalant bare-breasted women suspended in a sort of fog that was almost blue.

I remember that in Johannesburg my parents took me out to see a theatre performance of *Irma la Douce*, under the impression that it was *Mother Goose*. I could not understand why a woman would want to stand outside all alone in the lamplight like that.

I remember walking through Barbés after evening violin lessons, past the men gambling on upturned cardboard boxes in the street light, and the queue of immigrants outside a brothel where women stood behind a window with a dirty wire grille.

I remember the Indian man who used to go into restaurants at night near where I lived in Paris, selling basketfuls of roses. He had a woman's lips, and wore a rose behind one ear.

I remember reading that Brassaï once knocked at the door of a top floor flat in a building he had never entered before, because he wanted to take photographs of Paris by night from the window. The old man and woman who opened the door to him both turned out to be blind.

I remember queues of foreigners at broken public telephones in the middle of the night, waiting to call overseas for free.

I remember how many Tunisian cafés there used to be in the middle of Paris, open at all hours, selling sugary pastries; rolls with salad, tuna, hard-boiled eggs and harissa; and hot sweet mint tea.

I remember the silence of the riot police, standing astride all roads leading into the Bastille one night, with helmets and plexiglass shields, preventing motorcyclists from meeting there. Photographs of police clubbing anti-Algerian war protesters outside the Charonne metro station in 1962. And the gendarme who went into a telephone booth to make a call one evening. In the plastic lining of his képi there was a photo of a girl.

I remember the round, pasty-faced Japanese painter who lived in the flat below mine, letting out screams at night which were as thin and penetrating as syringe needles.

I remember the blonde hair of a girl burning on a pillow in a charcoal-dark room, while through the window the winged Genie de la Bastille balanced above the rooftops.

*

I REMEMBER how we were driving off in grey rainy weather from Paris to the town of Hirson (best known for its train station where lots of Picardy railway-lines intersect). We were on our honeymoon, two years after getting married. Suddenly all the cars on the road seemed to be going more slowly than we were.

I remember how we were flagged down by some previously invisible traffic cops for speeding. We had been driving at fifty kilometres an hour. The speed limit, as I soon discovered, was thirty.

We were ushered into a navy-blue van at the side of the road. There was a policeman wearing glasses sitting behind a typewriter at the far end. He was too big for his desk, and was looking very tense, as if expecting us to put up a nasty fight. In France, motorists often put up a nasty fight.

My wife started laughing. This was because on our wedding night she had also been in a car that was stopped by a traffic cop. Her laughter came out in generous, nervous peals, but it did not soften up the policeman, who looked more and more puzzled: we were not putting up the resistance he had been bracing himself for.

I was a few paces behind my wife. My hands were cold, and I wasn't breathing properly. I just wanted to get the whole incident over as rapidly as possible.

Later, I kept on having visions of my father, arrested at a road-block outside Durban. I imagined a deep crack running through the tar, and the cosmos in full brilliant bloom along the side of the road. The police must have asked him to identify himself. He would have gone red, then ashen. In the end, he would have handed the car keys over to the woman he was driving back to Johannesburg. He wasn't going to need them for a long long time.

I remember the town of Hirson, with its hotel that could have been anywhere. The Hirson supermarket and the Hirson Chateau. The overcast skies and intermittent rain. The museum with its disparate exhibits, including some photographs of Jews being rounded up and deported. Elsewhere, there was a list of possible origins of "Hirson" including "herisson" (hedgehog).

I remember the local newspaper, with a front-page article about a woman helping people in an old-age home to remember their past. The headline read "LA MEMOIRE EST UN MUSCLE": Memory is a muscle.

*

I REMEMBER that there was no one else in our Paris flat. The TV was to the right when you came in; I switched it on immediately, sinking into an old leather armchair without taking off my jacket. I remember that it was a Sunday, quite late in the afternoon. I had already been out earlier, sitting in front of another TV set with friends. On the screen I had seen the empty road in front of the prison; a crowd gathered in the glare and dust, the pressure of the crowd like water quietly accumulating against a wall. There were media teams and police and marshals, a treeful of people trying to get a better view, a man in an animal skin doing a pert, snappy dance in the middle of all the waiting. I remember "Why are we waiting, it's getting aggravating"; "They also serve who stand and wait"; and "Patience is a virtue, virtue is a grace; Grace is a virgin who never washed her face." I remember waiting for my turn at the barber's in a terrible silence of snipping upstairs at the O.K.Bazaars, and waiting for a girl called Cheryl to decide whether or not she would come out of her room and receive me when I went to invite her to our matric dance. The whole flat seemed to go tiptoeing around the entrance hall while I stood there in a state of hopeless anticipation. I remember the winding queue that seemed to be stuck in cement outside the pass-office on the west side of town. I remember the long bone-dry white thorns of the wag-'n-bietjie bos. I remember the hours I spent waiting for my father to arrive home after being released from prison, with the sun beating down on the thin half-bleached grass of our garden. I remember that the light started falling across Paris. The air smelt of rain. Our white chiffon curtains were being blown into the darkening flat, and I neither closed the windows nor switched on the light. I remember listening to the cars outside, extending our road into the distance like a strip of sizzling hot oil. I sat in a state of local anaesthesia wanting only to catch another flash of Mandela walking free, from one TV channel to the next. I remember that there was going to be dancing in the streets of Paris that evening, but I was going nowhere, Paris was nowhere and I was at the edge of the road outside Victor Verster prison in Paarl where Mandela appeared once more holding his fist up high, a clenched torch that had not yet unfurled its flame. The more he walked, among the slow-stepping clan-members, old cronies, strangers and heirs, the less he came closer, still withheld by the backwash of twenty seven years of absence, wrapped in the remoteness of the heat-warped air. Such an egg absence is, with a shell that grows bone-thick over the years and takes as many years again before it can be broken by the absent man balled up inside, while those outside knock and are hardly heard. I remember the moment on the *Movietone News* when the two teams digging the Mont Blanc tunnel met in the middle and you could see the laughter of their faces in the darkness. I remember my father, on the night after his release, standing at my open bedroom door as if he had not been granted the key to enter. Nor was I able to grant him that key. I remember when Mandela entered his car, and the road started moving tenuously, the tar mobile at last, stretching, lengthening under the tread of the tyres, forwards and backwards, across the confinement of the land.

*

I REMEMBER stop streets in Johannesburg. I remember walking along the icing-smooth white letters of the word STOP and being ordered back onto the pavement by my nanny. I remember roads that were rough-backed with feldspar chips sticking out slightly in the middle but smooth with little wrinkles at the sides where the tar had run into the gutter and you could roll it into balls as big as ghoens. I remember my brother with other children doing a tightrope-dance across the floor while singing "One little elephant balancing, step by step on a piece of string; he thought it such a jolly stunt that he called up another little elephant". I remember the special cordoned-off section of the Rand Easter Show where children could ride little cars, maybe go-karts, along painted roads, and learn traffic signs. I remember a film we saw at school, with death in a black cloak floating at the crossroads, stalking people who disobeyed traffic rules. I remember that I failed my driving test twice, the second time because I knocked something over when I tried to park; and also the long line of wheeler-dealers and desperate second-timers standing in line for roadworthy certificates for cars of dubious origin. I remember photographs in the newspaper that showed exactly where some drama had occurred by reproducing a photograph of a road with little black arrows on it pointing in various directions. I remember black male prisoners being herded along the road in Pretoria. I remember people "skipping the border" in cars and on motorbikes, and Goldreich and Wolpe who made it disguised as priests. I remember Canned Heat singing *Going up the country* at Woodstock, and Joni Mitchell singing "We are stardust, we are golden, and we've got to get ourselves back to the garden". I remember returning to South Africa after our family had left, opening the newspaper on someone's lawn, reading about unrest in a nearby township, and having the old feeling that what was happening out there was almost too remote to be real. I remember watching riot police throwing canisters of tear-gas at protesters under the plane trees on a wide boulevard off the place de la République in Paris. I remember the feeling of delight that people could actually be waltzing to an accordion in the street, despite all the crackers, on the fourteenth of July. I remember a taxi-driver asking me which country exactly I came from in South Africa. I remember one of the first questions French people used to ask me about South Africa: what kind of food do people eat there; what is your national dish? I remember many French people, as soon as they heard I came from South Africa, wanting to tell me exactly what *they* thought about the place. I remember not really wanting to talk about South Africa at all. I remember being in a room with some French people, and some South Africans who could not speak French, and being reluctant to speak a word of English. I remember travelling in a taxi, on the way from one TV set to another on the day Nelson Mandela was released from jail, and saying to the Tunisian taxi-driver: "I'm from South Africa", then repeating it just in case he hadn't heard me the first time.

*

I REMEMBER walking through the streets of Grahamstown, on a visit back to South Africa. The bite of winter in the air. All the beggars stalking me, with comfortable smiles and stories of hardship that could not possibly be untrue.

I remember learning not to sit writing at a table facing a window onto the street, otherwise there would be people knocking at the door every ten minutes asking for alms.

I remember the township, on a hillside facing the town like the other half of a hinge.

I remember the woman walking with some determination towards me. More than twenty paces away I already knew that I would not be able to refuse her.

I remember the slack smoothness of her cheeks, missing teeth, knotted doek; the skin of her arms and legs with that bleached edge to the blackness, as if they had been rubbed with salt. There was a whiff of cheap alcohol on her breath. Her glance was bright and sharp as a broken bottle.

She wanted money for groceries, she told me. So I said O.K., lets go to the supermarket.

I walked down the aisles picking up potatoes, oil, sugar. She tailed me discreetly.

I could already imagine the potatoes boiling in a pot; they sat in their bag on the way to the till, waiting like her hunger, just for a moment linking our alien lives.

I remember the look in her eyes as she received them: lean and dry, switching away from me as she considered the next step.

*

I REMEMBER arriving one evening at a house shared by a few friends in Durban. It was my first visit back to South Africa.

I don't remember at which moment the woman looked at me, or how I knew. But it happened in the kitchen, after dinner.

I went out later, and knocked at her door: she was staying in the garage round the back. She told me to come in quickly. This was, after all, against the law.

There was a candle burning. She had a mattress on the floor.

I don't remember being frightened, or not wanting to be there, or urgently needing to do what had to be done. Something in me went out to her, to the beauty in her face. And something shrank entirely, a vein of ice between the thighs.

I remember how much there was of her. Her desire, then gradual withdrawal as she sensed my blood changing direction.

I remember being in a car the next morning, dropping her off at work. She was wearing a cleanly starched nurse's uniform.

I got out of the car to say goodbye. She looked at me as if I was less than a stranger; more like something in a plastic bag that it would have been far better to leave in the deep-freeze.

*

I REMEMBER that the last time I offered anyone Rooibos tea at my parents' London home, it was to a group of South African men who gave me a collective dirty look because as political prisoners they had all drunk nothing but "that stuff" day in and day out.

I remember that the last time I heard my father talking about the political situation in South Africa, it was in a London hospital, to two pretty women who were giving him a physiotherapy session.

I remember that the last time I went back to the house in Johannesburg where I had spent my adolescence, I decided never to go again. Our giant tree, the one with pale wood soft as a book, had been chopped down. The house itself had undergone so much plastic surgery that it was altered beyond recognition.

I remember that the last time I drove my own car in South Africa it was to carry a young maple tree to the school where I had been teaching, so that it could be planted in the playground. Before leaving, I had locked up the tree in the car for too long in full sunlight, so the air in there had a gaseous, suffocating smell of chlorophyll.

*

> I remember how we went walking up the mountain slope at Kirstenbosch, my brother and sister, Myrtle Berman and I.

It was a cool, overcast afternoon, the air slightly moist and aromatic with the leaves of shrubs and plants. The paths changed from cobblestone to gravel as we reached a higher plane, above the gardens and ancient, green-bladed, leaning trees. In places, stiffly hatched wire fencing cut harshly against the slopes of winter vegetation. I remember all the discussions with my mother about where exactly we should scatter my father's ashes, since there was no place anywhere in South Africa which we could readily call his own. Nowhere, apart from prison, was the memory of his presence so rooted that we could return there with his remains now. My brother carried the brown plastic urn. My sister was the last to leave the silver-leaf tree we chose, dusting off the grass after we had finally tilted the urn and sifted out its contents, which were grey-white and filled with grit, not at all feathery as ash. I remember Myrtle Berman dressed in a pastel tracksuit, as if we were going to jog to the highest summit with my father's memory. I remember sleeping over at the home of Myrtle Berman and her family as a boy, and needing the light on in the passage. I remember hoping to see, from the silver-leaf tree where we scattered the ashes, the harbour from which our family had left Cape Town on my father's release, but this was not possible. I remember the cremation in Golders Green, the box sliding away, the flames we did not see. I wanted a burial, not a cremation. I remember dreaming that there was going to be a burial but there was no body, and instead of going towards the freshly dug grave, the mourners surrounded me. I remember my father standing in the Johannesburg bus that a friend had had installed in his garden as a hothouse, with seedlings from Kirstenbosch taking root in well-ordered pots. I remember how that friend went half-crazy with fear that he might be arrested for long-terminated political activity. Not long afterwards, in Pretoria Local, my father became the prison gardener. I remember how we all walked down-slope in the falling light, with variant shades of green and bruised grey below us. Later, we sat down together to a meal at Myrtle Berman's well-spread table. I remember that we had unknowingly picked a female tree. The bark seemed to bind the limbs of the branches tightly with its cracked metallic sheen. The light silver fuzz of the leaves was like a cat's shaved belly to the touch. The three cones that I brought back to France opened out a few months later; one day I found the seeds like small amber-winged insects burst across the surface of my desk.

*

I REMEMBER a South African writer speaking in a public library in one of the rougher suburbs of Paris, and then being verbally harassed by a group of adolescent girls. They did not appreciate the ending of one of her short stories, in which the Coloured narrator has an abortion after conceiving a child with a young white man. The girls badly needed the narrator to keep the child. The writer held up against them with the firm grace of a queen.

I remember three South African writers being invited to the drinks table during a reception at a smart Paris hotel, and all of them edging away like scared horses because they were on the wagon.

I remember a South African writer making such a wreck of his Paris hotel room after a drinking binge that the management had to completely redo the decor.

I remember six South African writers in their air-conditioned hotel rooms, languorously watching the fireworks from their windows on the eve of the fourteenth of July, with the tip of the Eiffel Tower just visible in the background.

I remember a South African theatre director informing his Paris audience that one of his first sources of inspiration was Tarzan.

I remember a South African writer in jeans and velskoene, slung across the luggage on his trolley at Roissy airport while waiting for me to pick him up. He looked as if he was riding through the veld on the back of a bakkie.

I remember a South African writer who hadn't been home for too long carefully unpacking a box of exotic seeds that had been collected for him in the fynbos by some friends.

I remember a South African writer asking me in a matter-of-fact way: "So, are you a resident here now, Denis?" We were in the middle of the city where I have lived for more than thirty years, and I suddenly felt as if I was going through customs.

*

I REMEMBER the voice of the woman as she read her poetry, sweet and raw and gritty as the inside of a fig.

I remember the way she read her poetry at a venue in Cape Town, with heavy maroon drapery behind her, the atmosphere in the room as inconsequential as tea-time, the urgency of her lines absorbed by the audience as if everyone were politely chewing sponge-cake.

I remember her reading her alphabet primer out on the veranda of her home, raised between the flat blue sea and the rusty heights of Table Mountain:
    Aardvark, armadil, alikreukel, akkedis;
    Buffel, brontosaurus, bokmakierie, blaasopvis.

I remember the windblown stroke of hair against her features, sunlight melting her glasses.

I remember that the owners of her Cape Town house had decided to "leave the country until things settled down".

I remember that when I phoned to invite her to Paris for a translation workshop she asked me to hold on a moment because she had just been out in the garden cutting dahlias and her hands were sticky.

I remember her walking out along the road near the mediaeval abbey where the workshop was taking place. She had been reporting for the Truth and Reconciliation Commission. Her hair had had the darkness shocked out of it and was now another colour.

I remember that once I woke up in Paris to see the living ash from a nearby fire come drifting past the window. Her hair reminded me of that colour.

I remember that we came to a quaint old stone house at the edge of the woods. There were carved wooden eaves, and diamond windowpanes with roses opening against them. The place was so still it was trembling, like a reflection in a lake. She stood there quietly, dousing herself.

*

I REMEMBER when it seemed that a whole village-full of people from Centr'Afrique had come teeming across the shiny lino tiles of the terminal at Roissy Airport. I was there to fetch my mother-in-law, but before I could find her they were already parading before me, slowly wading into the bass drone of the expectant crowd. There was a mother bending to direct her two small, immaculately dressed children, their faces gleaming like marbles, towards a giant of a man who tweaked each of their ears. Then she straightened and hitched a brown print dress back up over the boulder of her hips. There was a studious-looking man leading an old woman whose sockless, chapped feet were much too narrow for her new shoes. She kept her head down, as if the faces of the crowd would burn her. There was a middle-aged constantly smiling woman who punted herself along with a cane while the bright blue words across her orange dress sang the praises of Jesus. There were several single men in suits, each of them glowering, possibly because the plane had arrived hours late. There was a bouquet of young girls, each of their hairdo's bound with bits of yellow tape; a tiny girl lying on her back in the top compartment of a luggage trolley like a freshly unwrapped doll, big eyes dilated with wonder. There was a woman squeezed as tightly into her long, frilly-edged dress as stuffing into sausage skin, sweating under a bronze-tinted wig. As yet hardly descended from the sky, with a whiff of woodsmoke and sweet face-lotion, they came through the chrome mandibles of the doors beyond the customs zone; from there across the cold sterile length of the concourse. Amongst them, there was a man in his twenties, wearing a spotless white suit, a silver and black diagonally striped tie with a broad knot lodged at the throat of his starched collar. He had high cheek-bones above which his eyes seemed sunken in absence. Next to me in the waiting crowd, a man of about his age, who had been keeping a careful watch on the newly-arrived passengers, called out in a soft, hesitant voice: "Monsieur... Albert?" The other, taken out of his reverie as he walked past, answered with a blank voice and dry shake of the head: "Non". I remember that I was planning to go to South Africa later that year; I had not been back for years. I stood there with the hollow note of the man's voice in my mind, imagining my arrival at Jan Smuts Airport and someone calling out my name. I would answer "No" as I walked past because it was not really me, in South Africa I now had no name, I was blank as a gap between old floorboards, lean as a frontier at the far edge of the land.

WE WALK STRAIGHT SO YOU BETTER GET OUT THE WAY

FOUR

This had happened while they were still alive, and they were still alive and this had happened.

Nancy Huston

To live in the place where your grandfathers lived. Imagine.

Karen Press

*The eternal mystery of oars
that strike back while the boat floats forward;
thus actions and words strike back the past
so the body can move on with the man inside.*

Yehuda Amichai

Liquidate your stocks.

Frederico Fellini

I REMEMBER sitting on a bus on the way to a Habonim camp in Rustenburg, watching the girls with glossy hair and very invisible breasts whom I dreamed of kissing, and the boys who always got them first.

I remember the friend who leaned over to me and said something like "Don't worry, Denis, your time will come."

I remember falling ill with tonsilitis towards the beginning of the camp and pretending to be asleep when a freshly-formed couple came energetically whispering into the dormitory in the middle of the day.

I remember the young adults in charge of us going over the story of Moses in Egypt, and then inviting us to take wire and clay, or anything else that happened to be lying about, and find some way of representing the idea of freedom. We worked in small groups, making figurines that we hoped would look like slaves heaving blocks of stone; slave-masters with whips; Moses pointing his rod imperatively beyond the Red Sea.

I REMEMBER one girl who worked on her own, suspending a long-winged cardboard butterfly from a curve of wire and setting it in motionless flight. I hadn't really noticed her before: she was retiring and almost smouldering with shyness. For a long time after that, she was the one whom I dreamed of kissing.

*

I REMEMBER a dream in which I was standing in a birdcage filled with brilliantly coloured birds, and feathers came wafting down around me. I stooped to pick up a particularly beautiful one, and found myself flying out of the cage.

I remember that birdcage, the real one: it stood in the grounds of a mansion belonging to the family of one of my friends.

I remember my friend's mother looking daringly attractive in a pair of black stockings, without shoes, on the stage of our primary-school hall: she was in a production of *Blithe Spirit* with some other parents. Her nickname was "Tickey". She participated in lift-schemes, and the Tombola stand at our school fête, and the P.T.A. (which I at first thought was a group of parents and teachers who did Physical Training together).

I remember how proud she was of her garden, which was once the *Rand Daily Mail* Garden of the Month, or was at least photographed on the front page. The gardener was always out there in his blue overalls, watering and weeding.

I remember that if you came out of that garden and turned left, you reached the War Memorial, where an angel rose above the entrance with a beehive under one wing. A little further along was the zoo: the anxious panther and cigarette-puffing orang-outang, the monkeys waiting to catch monkey-nuts which you could buy in little brown paper bags and try to lob through the black bars of the cages, past the sign that read "PLEASE DO NOT FEED THE MONKEYS".

I remember that if you came out of the garden and turned right, you arrived at a red brick-faced block of flats where my great aunt Essie lived the last years of her life. She had a room in a flat belonging to her sister-in-law Bessie.

I remember several other places where Essie had lived before, always in other people's houses or flats, in small, meticulously kept rooms that were easy to vacate at a moment's notice.

I remember that she had once suffered an unnameable deception at the hands of a man whom no one would talk about. Now she worked as a secretary in the middle of town. In the evening she would drive up to my grandmother's or wherever else I was in her Fiat with running-boards and stalk-eyed headlamps, and ferry me home. Over the weekend, she took me and my grandmother to Rhodes Park, or the Balalaika Restaurant, the Zoo Lake or the Zoo.

I remember her Rothman's cigarettes and the tubes of veins along the back of her hand. The bevelled clear blue lozenge of the ring on her finger. The line of her body, slim and elegant as a seedpod suspended from the branch of a tree.

I remember one winter when we both happened to be in Durban, and I was dropped at her beachfront hotel. She was sitting alone, having breakfast. We went off together onto the cold and near-deserted beach, she started reading the newspaper, and then everything froze. On the front page was a headline announcing that my father had just been arrested.

*

I REMEMBER sitting in our history class at high-school and watching the black man come in bearing the register. The register was a long, soft-covered book as big as a ledger. The man, known as a "boy", was dressed in blue overalls and tackies.

I remember how he always passed the register to the teacher with an almost imperceptible bow, then retired to the corridor just outside the door while waiting for the register to be "taken". Afterwards, he came back in to collect it. He walked softly in his tackies, which were not very white.

I remember how it seemed to me that you could see raw rump-steak through the skin of our history teacher's cheeks. He also had long teeth, which emerged separately from each gum. They had a yellowish glint, like the side of a mealie pulled out of steaming water, when he smiled.

I remember expecting him to teach us something interesting. Maybe during the next lesson. Or the one after that.

I remember that the first poem I ever wrote was about the man who brought in the register, how he came around to each classroom with a book to record our presence, while he himself was absent from our lives. I don't remember anything of the poem itself, except that the language was fuzzy and wistful.

I remember writing draft after draft across the pages of an exercise book, in an emotional stew which must have had something to do with my father's absence.

I remember that, in a way, the history teacher reminded me of my father. They could both flare into a blind temper. The history teacher also had a hint of my father's passion, but he seemed to put most of it into cricket.

*

I REMEMBER us all entering the afternoon history class, and sitting at those sloped, gouged wooden desks: the boy from Greece with rosewood cheeks and diabetes; the sarcastic one from Moçambique with a brass ring on his finger; the bony Afrikaans one wearing a Band Aid across the moustache he was cultivating for the matric dance. There was the boy with bloodshot spaniel eyes who lost his girlfriend to the slick new arrival from Yugoslavia, and said his parents didn't want servants because they stank. There were jollers and day-dreamers, bullies and schloeps, all ducking in unison as History came over us once more with its thick noise of reinforced concrete being poured down a chute, an endless, stony, scratchy announcement falling hoarse as a sergeant-major, fact upon fact against the dull drum of the ear: Potgieter, Sarel Cilliers, Vegkop, Kaffir Wars, Dingaan, Mzilikazi, "bulalani abatagati!", Maritz and Pretorius, pledges and covenants, landdrosts, heemraden, D'Urban and Lord Carnarvon, wagons and rifles, bibles and blood, Rhodes, Beit, Barnato and the Jameson Raid, Kruger standing against the uitlanders with his one thumb and that torn grey bib of a beard; pipes of diamonds and seams of gold, red fins of dust rising as the diggers entered the darkness of the ground. Kruger was gone but six decades later we got Verwoerd, then Vorster, still trying to dam the rising tide of millions, building walls across a land of last ditch stands, reinforced concrete slabs of words against all the apertures of our history class. I remember the boy with acne boiling on his face and the flax of his hair from Holland, and another from Portugal with olive skin and an enigmatic grin. I remember them out on the sports field with the rest of us when the final bell had mercifully rung, one burning across hurdles, the other arching lean as hose-pipe water over the high-jump bar, more of us letting off steam on the rugby field, hockey field, cricket pitch, all the busy maps of our blood on the loose and behind us a still itching trail of Settlers and migrants, battle-gashed mercenaries, wanderers whose names were confiscated at customs, merchants, riff-raff, refugees, chancers, each with a suitcase of ancestors, a home-made jacket of dreams and shoe-laces of hope, the memory of a trek still lodged in the arch of the foot; and little of all this in our history book which was shut in the shadow at the bottom of our bags, out on the sidelines as we went swerving, dodging, weaving across open ground, ready or not for the next step.

*

I REMEMBER asking my father to help me with my map of the Great Trek. An expression of distaste filled his face, but he drew the map beautifully. Each of the trekker trails looked as if it had been left behind by a different kind of insect crossing fine wet sand.

I remember sitting for a long time at the side of a sand road watching an ant struggling to escape from the conical trap of an ant-lion.

I remember that a friend of mine who lived at the edge of the veld made a map of a huge stretch of fields, marking out the places where he had found different kinds of beetles.

I remember how, if you wanted to find a book showing pictures of an African tribe in a bookshop, you had to look in the section marked FLORA AND FAUNA.

I remember singing "This land is your land, this land is my land" at Habonim camp, and wondering exactly which land and which people we were singing about.

*

THESE DAYS, whenever I can, I sit down and set out for the South Africa I come from. Word by word, I cross the wide zigzagging fault-line in the field of time. In less than a sentence, I have arrived.

It is the mid-nineteen-sixties, at a holiday camp in the hills of Rustenburg, and some young teenagers have been asked to illustrate the idea of freedom. They are down on all fours building pyramids.

Figurines of slave-masters flick their whips at slaves yoked to great stones. Moses wields a miraculous rod. A butterfly goes vaulting through the air on its slender arc of wire.

Most of these teenagers have roots in South Africa that run only two or three generations deep. Behind them lie European stories of ghetto life and near annihilation which often go untold by their elders, the terror of them best forgotten. The old world is so remote in this easy, benevolent sunshine. The children of the survivors are elsewhere now, if not exactly in paradise then quite nearby: at the southern tip of Africa, a place their ancestors surely did not dream of; a place of forgetting.

This, for the moment, is where they set the compass of their selves, though many of them will not grow old in South Africa. Can they feel the flight in their young bones already? They will live out an old migrant story, bearing with them the founding myths of their past, repeating the story of Moses to their children like a lever that keeps them ready to roll onwards. They are the Hebrews, unsettled once more, heading for the next frontier, true to their name which means, among other things, Those Who Pass Over.

Every year they wrap up their unleavened bread and set off at the crack of dawn for another country. But not my father. He walks out after dinner, his mind filled with questions of freedom in the country where he lives, the soles of his shoes caked with Underground earth. One day I learn that he will not be coming home, and my mind goes dizzy with loss.

I see him falling, broad green branches of the plane trees turning like spokes above the glow of his bald head, grey flannel trousers fluttering, wings of his handsome moustache tightly closed; right past our house he plummets, down an empty shaft in the solid blue air, into a stink of darkness with a slop bucket in the corner and a pallet on the floor.

Moses and his people trek onwards, the devastated land of Egypt behind them, milk and honey ahead, while my father is locked into a prison cell. For years on end he stays there and I eat of his astringent absence, shot through with the sweetness of a dream; even now I chew on the seeds of return.

*

I remember my mother rushing out of the door in her white coat in the morning and my father leaving for a walk after dinner and not coming back. I remember how much time there was at night with no parents and a bored maid gazing at a wall in the kitchen. I remember when the bird in my dark chocolate cuckoo clock got stuck and let out a dry squawk. I remember lying in bed tracing a figure-eight with my big toe against the upper sheet, and thinking about something I seemed to have thought about before but that dissolved as I lay there thinking about it. I remember my father calling out "Durban time" in a low sing-song voice to wake me up in the half-light so we could all go on holiday. I remember "What's the time?" "Time you got a watch"; "What's the time? Half past my freckle", and "What's the time? Half past nine, Hang your broekies on the line". I remember learning that in the time it takes to say "one hippopotamus" slowly, a second has gone by. I remember watches with a thin red second hand; watches that told you on the back how many jewels there were inside, and waterproof watches that weren't. I remember watches with a little window for the day and another one for the date that was always wrong. I remember our teacher asking us how long we thought our bones would last. I remember "The worms crawl in, the worms crawl out, They crawl in thin and they crawl out stout, Awoo ahee, awoo ahee, ahappy we will be". I remember when we went to a funfair and the Zulu watchman came up and told us everything was closed because Strydom had just died. I remember an Afrikaans song on the radio with an accordion and a man singing all the months of the year in a jovial voice that sounded as if he had just had a lot of beer and a braai. I remember the four o'clocks growing among the blackjacks near our back fence. I remember discovering what "five o'clock shadow" meant and looking at men to see if they had any on their faces. I remember the problem of finding a man who would teach me how to shave. I remember prefects on gate duty, and late detention. I remember the teacher who used to tell us we would be late for our own funeral. I remember 90 day detention, and 180 day detention. I remember when people were reading Arthur Koestler's *Darkness at Noon*. I remember the *Sunrise, Sunset* song in *Fiddler on the Roof*, with the line "Is this the little girl I carried?" I remember my mother telling me how she was on her way home from medical school and I came rushing up the road to meet her. I remember listening to Bob Dylan singing "Time passes slowly when you're searchin' for love", and wondering why, if he was right, time seemed to be passing so quickly for me. I remember The Byrds singing "To everything, turn, turn, turn, There is a season, turn, turn, turn, And a time to every purpose under heaven." I remember Donald Campbell and his Bluebird, Paul Nash with his smooth brown hair, licking everyone in the world at 100 yards until something went wrong with his bones, and Stirling Moss who had such an unlikely surname for a racing driver. I remember when I was about to fall in love for the first time, and the girl in question was wearing trousers, sitting cross-legged under a table and talking to a girlfriend at a party in someone's Johannesburg flat. I remember that when I met the woman I was going to marry, the first thing we talked about was our grandmothers. I remember the sound of our daughter's heart, audible thanks to a monitor in the delivery room before she was born, like a horse that was softly pounding with great speed towards us.

THANKS

We Walk Straight So You Better Get Out The Way came directly in the wake of my previous book, *I Remember King Kong (the Boxer)*, but it soon took on a shape of its own. I wrote the text in the first section about the three boys who are called to the secretary's office, for a friend of mine, Antoine Fraisse. On seeing it, Adine Sagalyn pointed out that I had the form for a new book, and this is it.

On 17th May 2005, St. Patrick's Day, several of us did a reading of *I Remember King Kong (the Boxer)* at Odile Hellier's fine, welcoming Paris bookshop, The Village Voice: Vera Dickman, Nancy Huston, Declan McCavana, Tanith Noble and Adine Sagalyn. Mike Dickman sang. There was mention made of Joe Brainard and Georges Perec, whose respective books *I Remember* and *Je me souviens* lie behind both of mine. Also present was Maggie Davey, whose enthusiasm as my editor at Jacana has been precious fuel to me.

At a restaurant after that reading Vera Dickman beamed up at me from a table: "Do you remember 'We walk straight so you better get out the way' ?"

So I had a title, and then the text which begins "I remember how the girls would link arms like birds flying wing to wing" (hereby dedicated to her), which turned into the first of the series of lean trajectories crossing this book.

The first jottings of *We Walk Straight* were made at Marty Pato and Paula Singer's house in Villeneuve de Mézin; the book was also later completed there. Robert Berold arrived at the same house and did a meticulous critical reading of the initial manuscript. Not long afterwards, while I was at the nearby village of Le Fréchou watching the World Melon-pip Spitters' Championship, Stephen Clingman phoned up to give me further invaluable comments.

To all these people, to Isobel Dixon who found Jacana for me, as also to those friends who will recognise their doings in this book, great thanks.

REFERENCES

Inscriptions and general references:

Yehuda Amichai "The Eternal Mystery" in *Great Tranquility* New York: Harper and Row, 1983, tr.Glenda Abramson and Tudor Parfitt.

Robert Berold "the mirror" in *Rain Across a Paper Field* Durban: Gecko Poetry, 1999.

Frederico Fellini: untraced French magazine interview, late 1970's.

Nancy Huston "Erotic Literature in Postwar France" in *Raritan*, Vol. 12 No 1, Summer 1992.

Henri Michaux "Tranches de savoir" in *Face aux verrous*, Paris: Gallimard, 1992 (1951), tr. Denis Hirson.

Karen Press "Guess Who" in *Echo Location*, Durban: Gecko Poetry, 1998.

Wislawa Szymborska "No Title Required" and "May 16, 1973" in *Poems New and Collected* New York: Harcourt, 2000, tr. Stanislaw Baranczak and Clare Cavanagh.

Max Velthuijs *Frog and the Stranger* London: Andersen Press, 1995.

William Carlos Williams "The Descent" in *Collected Poems II, 1939-1962* Manchester: Carcanet, 2000.

*

p.25 A.A.Milne, "Disobedience" in *The World of Christopher Robin* New York: E.P.Dutton, 1958

p.36 limerick by Rudyard Kipling

p.82 Wopko Jensma, "Spanner in the What? Works" in *i must show you my clippings* Johannesburg: Ravan, 1977. Also, "Onder Ander" in *Sing for Our Execution* Johannesburg: Ophir/Ravan, 1973.

p.98 *Walkin' Down the Line* by Bob Dylan

p.130 Alphabet primer, unpublished, by Antjie Krog

ACKNOWLEDGEMENTS

Grateful acknowledgement is made to the following for permission to reprint previously published material:

Bad Monk Music: Excerpt from "One of Us Can't Be Wrong" by Leonard Cohen. Copyright © 1995. All rights administered by Sony/ATV Music Publishing, 8 Music Square West, Nashville, TN 37203. All rights reserved. Reprinted by permission.

Big Sky Music: Excerpt from "Time Passes Slowly" by Bob Dylan. Copyright © 1970 by Big Sky Music. All rights reserved. International copyright secured. Reprinted by permission.

Crazy Crow Music: Excerpt from "Woodstock" by Joni Mitchell. Copyright © 1973 by Crazy Crow Music. All rights administered by Sony/ATV Music Publishing, 8 Music Square West, Nashville, TN 37203. All rights reserved. Reprinted by permission.

Dwarf Music: Excerpt from "This Wheel's on Fire" by Bob Dylan. Copyright © 1967 by Dwarf Music. All rights reserved. International copyright secured. Reprinted by permission.

Editions Gallimard: Excerpt from "Tranches de savoir" in *Face aux verrous* (1951) by Henri Michaux © by *Editions Gallimard*, Paris. Reprinted by permission.

Egmont UK Limited: Excerpt from "Disobedience" by A.A.Milne in *When We Were Very Young* © A.A. Milne. Published by Egmont UK, London. Reprinted by permission.

Faber and Faber: Excerpts from "No Title Required" and "May 16, 1973" by Wislawa Szymborska, from *Poems: New and Collected 1957-1997* © by Faber and Faber, London. Reprinted by permission.

Ice Nine Publishing Company: Excerpt from "Uncle John's Band" by The Grateful Dead, lyrics by Robert Hunter. Copyright © by Ice Nine Publishing Company. Reprinted by permission.

Joni Mitchell Publishing Corp. : Excerpt from "A Case of You" by Joni Mitchell. Copyright © 1972. All rights administered by Sony/ATV Music Publishing, 8 Music Square West, Nashville, TN 37203. All rights reserved. Reprinted by permission.

Melody Trails, Inc. : Excerpt from "Turn! Turn! Turn! (To Everything There Is A Season) by The Byrds (words from the book of Ecclesiastes, music by Pete Seeger) © Melody Trails, Inc. Reprinted by permission.

The Estate of Wopko Jensma: Excerpt from "Onder Ander" in *Sing for our Execution*, Ophir/Ravan Press, 1973; excerpt from "Spanner in the What? Works" in *i must show you my clippings* Ravan Press, 1977, both © The estate of Wopko Jensma.

Warner Bros. Inc. and *Special Rider Music*: Excerpt from "Walkin' Down the Line" by Bob Dylan. Copyright © 1963 by Warner Bros. Inc. Copyright renewed 1991 by Special Rider Music. All rights reserved. International copyright secured. Reprinted by permission.

Wixen Music: Excerpt from "The Spy" by Jim Morrison. Copyright © by Wixen Music. Reprinted by permission.